REDBOOK

MOM'S
SURVIVAL
GUIDE

REDBOOK

MOM'S SURVIVAL GUIDE

SAVE TIME, MONEY, and YOUR SANITY

EDITED BY SUSAN RANDOL

HEARST BOOKS

A division of Sterling Publishing Co., Inc.

New York / London

www.sterlingpublishing.com

Contents

Foreword

I'm a mom, and since you've picked up this book, it seems a safe bet that you're a mom, too. And as you know, we moms get to live the good, the bad, and all the stuff in between. We get the hugs and kisses—and the sudden temper tantrum in public. The brilliant artwork—and the sleepless nights. The holiday traditions—and the homework struggles. And somehow we have to provide expert advice, emotional warmth, and our own personal touch to every bump along the way. Yikes! How on Earth do we even have the bravery to attempt all this?

Dip into *Redbook Mom's Survival Guide* and you'll find exactly what you need to guide you along this always exciting, sometimes challenging journey. Our experts give you helpful advice on dealing with everything from your child's food allergies and envy to their body image problems and puppy love. Plus, we've been listening to another band of experts on the way: you. So you'll also find tidbits from fabulous *Redbook* moms who have been there, done that, and are willing to tell you all about what works and what doesn't.

If you're a list lover like me, you'll particularly want to check out "5 Easy Ways to Get Your Kids to Eat Healthier," "7 Ways to Make Staying Fit Fun," "5 Symptoms Moms Can Relax About (And 4 to Never Ignore)," "14 Fun—and Memorable—Ways to Bond as a Family," and much, much more. I've found priceless information in these lists—and throughout this book—on eating right, staying safe, and so much more that I've already used as I raise, love, and enjoy my son.

But perhaps the most important advice for any mom is to take care of you: to carve out some "me time," to make sure that you keep your sense of humor and sense of self as you continue on this fascinating journey. In fact, the first section of this book concentrates on you—it helps you define yourself as a mom, acknowledges that being a mom often isn't easy, and shows you how to celebrate your strengths as a parent, even if you (or others!) doubt your abilities.

All moms want the best for their kids. You and I are no exception! And *Redbook Mom's Survival Guide* is the tool we need to craft the healthiest, safest, strongest, richest childhood for our kids—and for ourselves too. Won't you turn the page and start the journey with me?

STACY MORRISON
Editor-in-Chief, *Redbook*

Introduction

You conquered childbirth, mastered midnight feedings, organized bottles and binkies, and prevailed over potty training. You are a mom! And now you can sail through calm seas until adolescence, when the storms hit—right? Well, almost. Before you get there, you'll have to deal with the sometimes tumultuous and always exciting early years of childhood. What do you do when your kid will eat only white food? How should you handle a playdate tantrum? What should you do if your child's fear is turning into a phobia? Which symptoms mean you should take your child to the doctor right away? How can you get your kids excited about going back to school? You need to know what to do, how to do it, when to do it, and when to call in an expert.

This reassuring handbook is packed with vital information on how to navigate these uncharted waters. Here is advice from a wide range of experts—psychologists, doctors, teachers, experienced moms, and more—on subjects ranging from preventing illness to instilling discipline, from quelling sibling battles to creating family holiday traditions. Best of all, you don't need to read the book cover to cover to benefit from the wisdom within. Simply turn to the section that covers your immediate, particular concern, and you will find time-tested strategies and sanity-saving ideas to make even your most hassled days run a little more smoothly.

Whether you're a working mom, a stay-at-home mom, or a mom who has fashioned a life between the two, you're sure to recognize yourself and your children in the pages that follow. And no matter your parenting style, you'll find invaluable information from a trusted source, directly from the front lines of motherhood.

CHAPTER ONE

Moms

Motherhood is exhilarating and exhausting, wrenching and rewarding. It breaks your heart and mends your soul. Wouldn't it be great if the job came with directions? Here's the closest thing possible to a comprehensive job description: a quiz to determine your mom personality; a list of the five hardest things about being a mom; ways to reduce stress; tips for balancing work and home, (even if you work from home); strategies for celebrating your strengths as a mom; and lessons we can learn from our kids.

The Toughest, Best Job in the World

You may not get paid much—okay, you don't make a dime—but you have the most important, most influential job in the world. Here's advice on how to handle this job, tailored to your mom personality.

What's *Your* Mom Personality?

What defines you as a mom? Is it your crafty, do-it-yourself attitude or your knack for always being up for a little Dance Dance Revolution? Take this quiz to face—and embrace—your unique mom style.

1. **To celebrate Green Week at school, your son has to re-create the natural habitat of an animal on the endangered species list. He picks the Atlantic salmon. Your first thought when he brings home the assignment is:**
   a. You'd better think of something else to make for dinner.
   b. You already have everything he'll need—simulated riverbed rocks, plastic underwater plants, and sequins that look like scales.
   c. Camping and hiking! You definitely have to take the kids camping and hiking this summer.
   d. This project ought to be fun. You can't wait to see what he dreams up.

2. **You couldn't be more proud of your daughter for making the traveling field hockey team. This means you're going to have to:**

   a. go online and download the International Field Hockey Federation's rules of the game, just so you're up on the regulations.

   b. talk to her about saving her chore money to chip in for at least part of the $150 participation fee and the $100 uniform.

   c. swing by the craft store for some stickers, picture corners, and another pair of scallop-edged scissors for a field hockey scrapbook.

   d. buy some face paint and a giant foam finger in her team colors.

3. **When a lazy Sunday afternoon comes dangerously close to Mom-I'm-Bored Code Red, you:**

   a. pull out the art supplies and let their imaginations go wild.

   b. roll out the bicycles, in-line skates, and scooters and head to the nearest park.

   c. break out the video camera and tell them to put on a show.

   d. let the kids pick from the list above for an hour or two, then get back to your lazy Sunday afternoon.

4. **You've learned that the best way to grocery shop with the kids is to:**

   a. turn it into a game—give each child a list, then go aisle by aisle on a supermarket scavenger hunt.

   b. bring along a grocery kit (toys, video games, and snacks) for distraction.

   c. shop the store with those mammoth fire-truck shopping carts. They're impossible to maneuver and way too small to fit all your groceries, but it keeps everybody laughing.

   d. shop online, have the food delivered, and get your life back.

5. **After the kids are asleep, you usually:**

   a. download pictures from the camera to your Flickr account or update the family blog.

   b. get their lunches, backpacks, and gym bags ready for the next day.

   c. unwind and de-stress.

   d. check your e-mail and forward the jokes your friends and family have sent you.

6. **If we were to send a camera crew to your house on any weekday morning, it would look like an episode of:**
   a. *America's Funniest Home Videos*—From inadvertent soccer balls to the groin to milk from the nostrils, anything can happen in the span of an hour.
   b. *30 Minute Meals with Rachael Ray*—You've got less than 30 minutes to get them something healthy and, um, yum-o.
   c. *Supernanny*—But toward the end of the show, when the kids are calm, the parents are cool, and the naughty chair looms in the corner.
   d. *The Amazing Race*—From the time you get up until the moment they walk into school, it's a race against the clock.

7. **Your favorite minor holiday of the year is:**
   a. Halloween. Costumes, cupcakes, candy, and crafts—there's nothing better than dressing up in scary getups and making things in batches of 12.
   b. April Fool's Day. Practical jokes reign supreme and no one—not even Grandma or the baby—is safe in your house.
   c. Mother's Day. Sweet reciprocity.
   d. Super Bowl Sunday. Buffalo wings, chips and dip, and a little competitive fun.

8. **It's a triple-birthday-party weekend (you didn't realize when you RSVP'd yes to all three that they'd all occur within 48 hours of one another). You'd better:**
   a. call one of the hosts and tell them you have a conflict (with your mommy time) and hope she understands.
   b. get started on the birthday cards—handmade trinkets don't make themselves.
   c. stock up on hand sanitizer and gift cards—it's game time.
   d. get the ginger ale and hot water bottle ready—you're about to triple your pizza intake.

9. Speaking of birthday parties, you run across the perfect theme for your daughter's 9th birthday bash in a magazine. Once you download the templates for the invitations and favors, you realize it would probably be easier to put together a shelving unit from IKEA . . . blindfolded. You:

   a. go for it anyway—you want to make her special day memorable.

   b. scrap the idea and take her to the party store—more than 1,000 party themes to choose from.

   c. order a pizza and tell her to pull up a chair and grab a glue stick—this'll be a lot more fun assembly-line style.

   d. laugh at your misguided attempt to channel Martha Stewart, then log on and send funny Evites instead.

10. You're dealing with a pretty long face on the way home from a very disappointing Math League loss. The best way to cheer up your little guy is to:

   a. leave him alone for a while until he's ready to talk about it.

   b. explain that in every match there has to be a winner and loser, but loss doesn't have to mean defeat.

   c. tell him a surefire joke.

   d. dig right into the Win or Lose cupcakes you made before the contest.

SCORING

1. (a) 3 (b) 1 (c) 2 (d) 4
2. (a) 2 (b) 4 (c) 1 (d) 3
3. (a) 3 (b) 2 (c) 1 (d) 4
4. (a) 1 (b) 2 (c) 4 (d) 3
5. (a) 3 (b) 1 (c) 4 (d) 2

6. (a) 1 (b) 3 (c) 4 (d) 2
7. (a) 2 (b) 1 (c) 3 (d) 4
8. (a) 4 (b) 1 (c) 2 (d) 3
9. (a) 1 (b) 4 (c) 2 (d) 3
10. (a) 4 (b) 2 (c) 3 (d) 1

Turn the page to see your Mom Personality!

What's *Your* Mom Personality?

10–17 points The DIY Mom

Whether it's a diorama, a dozen cupcakes, or a quick haircut, there's nothing you can't assemble, whip up, or do. You turn what others think of as drudgery (90 brownies for the bake sale?) into activities that are fun and meaningful for both you and your kids. "DIY Moms are dedicated and talented—often the envy of other mothers," says Tammy Gold, a psychotherapist and parent coach. You thrill to the wonder and magic of childhood and want to put your stamp on those experiences for your kids. If you find yourself veering into perfection obsession, let your kids help out a little— the cake may be a little wobbly, but remember, they're learning from the best!

Who Am I?

"**I'm a DIY mom.** I make homemade baby food, I hand-knit baby blankets, and I make personalized Christmas cards. I'd love to do even more—but I do have to work for a living!"

18–25 points The ESPN Mom

Soccer, tae kwon do, ballet—these are just a few of the pursuits you manage to pack into after-school hours and weekends. You know the names of all your kids' teammates, have a special stopwatch you use to time splits, and other moms depend on you to let them know which team is winning, and, um, how the game works. You want your kids to experience everything life has to offer—and you derive deep satisfaction from knowing they have lots of choices. Make sure you leave some room in the schedule for your own passions—and remember, taking a break isn't just for slackers. "Rest and unstructured play is essential for kids," says Gold, "and moms too!"

Who Am I?

"**I am an ESPN mom.** On weekends we run from dancing to swimming to piano lessons. It's nonstop. We pack lots of activities in so Julia can have all the experiences she wants to have."

Who Am I?

"**I'm an LOL mom.** I defuse lots of situations with a joke, a poke, or a tickle. But it's hard to always know what's comical. If my son says, 'It's not funny!' then I have to dial it down."

26–33 points **The LOL Mom**

Fun reigns in your house. From knock-knocks to practical jokes, finding ways to make the kids laugh is the cure for whatever is ailing you and them. There's a lightness about your parenting, an effervescence that allows you to easily communicate your love for life to your kids. "Joy is a must when raising children," says Gold, and your ability to see the sunny side—even when clouds are passing over you—teaches your kids the art of resilience. But life can't be all fun and games: Your kids should know that the jokes stop once the rules are broken—and as long as you walk the line between fun and firm, handling the sensitive topics with care, they will.

Who Am I?

"**I'm a Wii Mom** because I let my son take the reins on things, from cooking to art projects. I'm always nearby if he needs me, but I also wait for him to ask before jumping in."

34–40 points **The Wii Mom**

Yep, just like the folks responsible for the addictive gaming system, you know that the real fun starts when you're standing side by side with—not hovering over—your child. You've encouraged your kid to be an independent thinker from her very first homework assignment. "Wii Moms want very much for their children to stand on their own two feet," says Gold. "And they have a strong sense of their own identity," which is why you set a great example for others on how to not lose yourself in the role of "Mom." Plus, granting your kids a little freedom means you get some too. Call it Mii time. Still, you're always there for guidance; he knows you're his biggest fan.

The 5 Hardest Things about Being a Mom

Motherhood is a major learning curve. One minute you're pregnant and the next you're an instant expert in basic infant first aid and child psychology. At the same time, you have to finesse the emotional hurdles of motherhood, especially when they morph and mutate as your child reaches each new milestone.

"In my 20 years of practice as a psychiatrist, I've noticed that there are certain things that we as moms skin our knees over time and time again," says Valerie Davis Raskin, M.D., author of *The Making of a Mother*. "If you can identify those emotional trials and learn from them," says Raskin, "you can apply that wisdom when they come up again."

That said, there's no one right way to cope with any of the five emotionally charged mom obstacles outlined here. But Raskin's advice will get you started on developing coping strategies that make these tough passages on the journey of motherhood easier to manage.

Mom Challenge #1 — When you don't like your kid

When your child misbehaves, or embarrasses or betrays you, it can make you so angry that you might even hate him for it (for about 10 minutes). And then, because you also love him, you immediately feel tremendous guilt.

HOW TO COPE: You're always going to have what Raskin calls "unloving thoughts" about your child. You may even lose your cool and say not-such-nice things. That's normal! "You're human and you need to have reasonable expectations of yourself," Raskin says. "Always being 100 percent in love with your child is not reasonable." But if you're having an overly emotional reaction to your kid's misstep, try to figure out what your upset is really about. Then, address that fear or anxiety directly, instead of taking it out on your kid.

What Was the Moment You First Felt Like a Mom?

"My 5-year-old daughter came home from school and told me that her favorite friend wasn't coming to her birthday party because we were going to serve doughnuts instead of cake. Her friend said, 'It's not a real birthday party.' Preparing myself for a moment of teaching and consoling, I asked my daughter how she felt. She responded, 'She's sure going to miss a fun party!' At that moment, I thought, I'm *this* kid's mom, and I'm so proud of her. I hope I had something to do with that."

Mom Challenge #2   Letting Dad parent, too

It's natural to want everything to be perfect for your kids, and the feeling that they depend on you completely can be downright intoxicating. So how do you share this awesome responsibility with Dad, who—in your opinion—lets them wear mismatched outfits (they'll be social outcasts!), tosses them in the air (he'll break their little necks!), and plays monster chasing them around (exactly when they should be winding down for sleep!) Who needs this kind of help? *You* do.

HOW TO COPE: "In this culture of perfectionism, it's easy to fall into the trap of 'If I don't do it, it won't get done right,'" Raskin says. But as frustrating as you may find Dad's fast-and-loose parenting style, recognize that it's actually a great change of pace for kids. "Kids want to be loved in different ways, and to experience different aspects of love," Raskin says. "As long as Dad's ways aren't dangerous, it's a good idea to let it go." Another motivation for making peace with your husband's parenting: When you refrain from criticizing his every move, you preserve a sense of mutual respect and harmony in your marriage. "Anything you do that strengthens the relationship of Mom and Dad is by definition good for children," says Raskin.

Mom Challenge #3   Separation anxiety (yours!)

For weeks, Kathie Papera dreaded her 4-year-old's first day of preschool. "I pictured her crying and holding on to my feet," says the Manhattan Beach, CA, mom. To her surprise, however, her usually shy daughter stopped acknowledging her mother's existence after about 10 minutes with her new teachers and friends. "At some point she ran up to me and whispered in my ear, 'It's okay, Mommy, you can go now,'" Papera says—so she slowly backed out of the room . . . and cried the entire drive home.

HOW TO COPE: For starters, recognize that your emotions are separate from your child's. "You have to know that what you're feeling is your own anxiety and sadness and not theirs," Raskin says. Even if your child is bawling and freaking out, you must realize two things: (1) He'll probably be fine 5 minutes after you leave (most kids are), and (2) the challenge of adapting to a new environment is one of those life experiences that will help him grow and develop. "If you block the separation, you end up fostering excessive dependency," Raskin says. "Remind yourself that your goal is to raise a happy, independent child." And when you break down in tears anyway—in spite of all the logical reasons not to—go sit in your car and have a good cry. "It's okay to feel sad. You're grieving the loss of your baby on some level, even if that baby is 18," Raskin says. "But by the same token, you get a little piece of your life back!"

Mom Challenge #4 **Accepting your child's failures**
You're dying for your son to swim competitively, but he's content to just take lessons; you hope your daughter will star as Annie, but she's cast as orphan number 12. When kids don't live up to your expectations (or even show interest in trying), you're bound to feel disappointed for them. But make no mistake—the deeper disappointment is the one you feel for yourself.

HOW TO COPE: All parents secretly hope their kids will earn an Olympic gold medal and graduate with top honors from Harvard, but most of *us* didn't do those things, so why should we expect them of our kids? "Your child is unique, with her own talents, dreams, goals, and perhaps problems that aren't as you wished them to be—whether because she has a disability, is quirky, or is just different from you," Raskin says. You'll both feel better if you can learn to express pride in things that are genuinely achievable for your child, emphasizing the effort that she's making.

A Mom's Worth: $841,900

That's what the annual salary would be for mothers if they were paid for all the work they do—from raising the kids to cooking, cleaning, and generally maintaining family harmony (not to mention one or two science projects thrown in along the way)—according to a 2009 Edelman Financial Services LLC study. Good thing motherhood is its own reward!

Mom Challenge #5 **Learning to let go**

We all want to keep our children safe from harm—it's arguably our number one job as parents. But it's easy to go overboard because those precious bundles are so vulnerable. After 9/11, Sue Donas was convinced that someone was going to pipe bomb her daughter's day care near Hillsdale, NJ, because it was housed in a Jewish community center. She used to circle the building looking for suspicious characters. Once she even had an abandoned car towed away. "I drove to work every day anxious that something terrible was going to happen to Ari," Donas says.

HOW TO COPE: "You can't raise your child in a bubble," Raskin says, "but you can get reassurance that she's in responsible, protective hands." For example, instead of patrolling the day care grounds, Donas could inquire about the school's security policy—and it might just set her mind at ease. "Never be embarrassed to get the information you need," says Raskin. There's nothing wrong with asking if all the lifeguards are certified or if the babysitter knows CPR. And if you don't like what you hear, make changes. "That eases your anxiety because it means you've done due diligence," Raskin says. "Once you've done all you possibly can, it's easier to let go."

Stress-free Mom = Healthy Kids!

A study from the University of Rochester has found that the more stressed a parent is, the more likely her child is to get sick—so taking care of your own mental health is like giving your kid a shot of vitamin C. Claire Michaels Wheeler, M.D., author of *10 Simple Solutions to Stress*, offers stressbusters for strung-out moms:

- **MORNING-ROUTINE MANIA:** When your kids are screaming, "Where's my backpack?" as you try to pack lunches without being late for your own meeting, take a moment to release the tension, says Wheeler. "Gather everyone together in a circle and pound on your chests and scream like Tarzan for 30 seconds," she says. "You'll all start laughing and start your day in a much better mood."

- **PTA-COMMITTEE OVERLOAD:** Instead of being guilted into doing everything from heading up the spring fair to sewing costumes for the school play, team up with a good friend and take on only those commitments you can do together. "That way, not only can you share the workload but it will also be a lot more fun," says Wheeler.

- **THE CONSTANT TO-DO LIST PLAYING IN YOUR BRAIN:** "Everyone always says to take a bubble bath to relax, but then you're just lying in the bubbles thinking about all the other things you should be doing while you're in the tub," points out Wheeler. Instead, choose an indulgence that engages your brain, like reading your favorite Jane Austen novel or picking up that Beatles piano book you learned to play 20 years ago, and find a half hour after the kids have gone to bed to enjoy.

Juggling Work and Home

It's more than a balancing act—it's an astonishing feat of juggling, keeping both your work and home lives running smoothly. Find out below how others have managed, whether they put in hours at a traditional workplace or work from home.

Work/Life Solutions That Work

Check out some of the innovative ways businesses and real women are supporting the needs and choices of *all* moms.

- **TRUE FAMILY LEAVE.** A program at Deloitte & Touche allows qualified employees to leave the company for up to five years to pursue a personal goal, such as raising children, getting a

Older Moms: Why It's Great to Wait

When Elizabeth Gregory became a mom for the first time at 39, she wasn't the only parent at the playground who could talk about Elmo *and* remember Elvis. But even though she is part of a growing trend—more than 8 percent of first children are now born to women over 35, compared with just 1 percent in 1970—she wasn't hearing much in the media describing how thrilled older moms were with their choice. "I could only find articles that talked about the difficulties—not the joys—of starting a family as you get older," says Gregory, a professor of women's studies at the University of Houston and the mother of two girls. She spoke to more than 100 women who had their first child after age 35 and reported her findings in her book, *Ready: Why Women Are Embracing the New Later Motherhood*. In addition to having higher salaries, more money saved, and stable relationships, Gregory writes that these moms felt ready to "move into a new phase of life, one that involved reveling in home life, including diapers, . . . homework, and responsibility. A big part of the later-motherhood story is plain old-fashioned family happiness."

degree, or tending to a sick family member. Candidates must resign from the company and not work during their years away, but they are guaranteed a job when they return—and in the meantime, they get hooked up with mentors, receive training and career coaching, and are invited to networking functions and company events.

- **BABYSITTING WITH A BONUS.** For 30 working and stay-at-home moms in Huntington Woods, MI, the local babysitting co-op is a lifesaver. Need to go to the hair salon for an hour? Call the bookkeeper, a position that is rotated among the members. She will call around until someone accepts the job. That mom acquires four points for taking care of your child. She will, in turn, use those points toward her own request. Besides the free babysitting, members also have a ready-made support system, says co-op member Lisa Kreinbring. "Some people have had serious illnesses and injuries, and all it takes is one e-mail and people set up to watch your kids, get you meals—it's a friendship thing."

- **FLEXTIME, REDEFINED.** Ever thought it would be great if you could work just during the school year and have summers off to spend with your kids? That's one of many flextime options for employees at Minnesota-based financial services company RSM McGladrey, along with telecommuting, job sharing, or creating a custom flexible work schedule to fit your needs.

- **DROP-IN CHILD CARE.** Texas moms in need of a few hours to run errands or just have lunch with the girls can drop their charges off at Kid Space, an indoor play space and child-care center. Parents use Kid Space for emergency backup babysitting or even in place of a regular sitter; homeschooling moms often use Kid Space to give their kids social time.

Real Advice from Real Moms

How do you cure the chronic lateness that comes from juggling work and home?

"I made an agenda for my boys that outlines their morning routine and ends with playtime. It's great incentive to stay on track with brushing teeth, getting dressed, and eating breakfast because if they finish everything, they get some time to play."

● **A ROOM OF ONE'S OWN.** New York City parents who want to keep a toe or two in the working world can find refuge at Two Rooms, where self-employed moms (and dads!) can use office space while child-care professionals look after Junior in the next room. The idea came to founder Elizabeth Kaiden 6 years ago, when the freelance writer and theater critic was adding "mom" to her resume. "As I got to know other parents, I found that we were all dealing with the same issues—we wanted to work some of the time to make money or keep our hand in, but we also wanted to take care of our children," recalls Kaiden, now a mother of three. "The choice between being a full-time employee or a full-time mom seemed too stark for people of my generation. I thought there had to be another way."

Who Plays Hooky When Junior Takes a Sick Day?

If you notice a distinct shortage of women in the office during cold and flu season, it's not necessarily because they're all in bed chugging cough syrup; they're probably home wiping someone *else's* nose. In a 2008 study, 78 percent of women in two-income families reported taking time off from work for urgent care—when a child is sick, school is closed, or child-care arrangements fall through—while only 27 percent of men did the same, according to research by David J. Maume, Ph.D., a professor of sociology at the University of Cincinnati. And it doesn't matter who's the bigger breadwinner: "By a large margin, women exceeded men in providing urgent care at all levels of income, as well as all levels of education," Maume says. Proof that no matter how much the world changes, moms will always be the best medicine.

Sanity Savers for Work-at-home Moms

A home-based business is a perfect fit for many moms—you can earn money and advance your career while arranging your schedule around playdates and soccer games. But trying to conduct a business call while your child is begging to sit on your lap can be tricky. We asked Bonnie Kelly and Teresa Walsh, cofounders of Silpada Designs, an at-home jewelry business, who've been working together since their oldest kids were in first grade (they're now 28), how to keep your home life from spilling into your home office, and vice versa.

- **SET REGULAR HOURS AND STICK TO THEM.** "Otherwise, you feel like you're working 24/7—but not actually accomplishing anything," says Kelly. "If you know you have between 2 P.M. and 6 P.M. on Thursday to work, then you crunch it out, and afterward there's no nagging guilt that you should be working when you're with your kids."

- **PLAN PROJECTS AROUND CHILD CARE.** There are some work tasks—stuffing envelopes, labeling packages—that you can accomplish with the kids around (they might even help!), says Walsh. But save business calls and focused work like writing for times when the kids are in school or with a sitter. Can't afford a sitter? "Swap a few hours of babysitting a week with another mom," she adds.

- **GIVE EVERYONE AN OFFICE.** Keep your desk from becoming a crayon and Barbie repository by giving your kids their own work tables. "While you are working, they can do their own 'work,' with stickers, ink pads, and Play-Doh," Kelly explains.

- **RESPECT YOURSELF.** Even if your work uniform is sweatpants and bare feet, you have to see yourself as a businesswoman. "When you take yourself seriously and convey that to your family and friends, then they will start to treat you that way and respect your boundaries," says Walsh.

How do you cure the chronic lateness that comes from juggling work and home?

"My kids wear their bathrobes to breakfast. Otherwise, something will spill, we'll have to get dressed all over again, and we'll never make it out the door on time."

"I always get gas on my way home at the end of the day so I don't have to waste time stopping when I'm expected somewhere in the morning."

Are You a Good Enough Mom?

Do you sometimes doubt your mothering abilities? Do others push you in that direction? It's time to stop doubting and start celebrating your strengths! The tips below will help you get the party started.

Why You're a Great Mom, No Matter How You Mother

Is there a right way to be a mom? Fortunately, parenting is not one-size-fits-all. "What works for one mom may not work for another—or her kids," says Michele Borba, author of *12 Simple Secrets Real Moms Know*. And it's important to get comfortable with *your* innate parenting style. "If you're always worrying—*am I doing it right?*—it could hinder your ability to parent effectively," says marriage, family, and child therapist Lisa Dunning, author of *Good Parents Bad Parenting*. "But if you trust yourself as a parent, you can focus on what's best for you and your child." What's more, feeling secure about your own style actually makes you a better parent—you're not constantly "trying on" other moms' methods, which can confuse your kids. "When you're confident and reliable in your parenting, kids know what's expected of them, and they learn to trust you and feel safe," Dunning says. Follow these five steps to get comfortable with your particular parenting style and make the most of it.

1. **STOP THE COMPARE-A-THON.** "Other people are our worst enemy when it comes to destroying our instincts," says Mary DeBiccari of Lake Grove, NY, who has two kids, 5 and 2, and a third on the way. "When a friend would say, 'You use wipes instead of washcloths?' and 'How could you not feed on demand?' I would second-guess everything I did." Try to tune out those unsolicited opinions. "When it comes to how your child adapts and copes and his unique emotional and physical needs, you're the expert," Borba says. "And when you go with what you know is right for your child, it will make you the best possible parent."

2. **TRACE THE ROOTS OF YOUR PARENTING STYLE.** No matter how hard you try to forge your own unique path as a mom, there's a good chance you're raising your kids the same way your parents raised you—for better and worse. "When you feel a little pain in your stomach because you've triggered a bad memory from growing up, it's a good sign that maybe this is one behavior you don't want to pass on to your kids," Borba says. One of the great gifts you get from being a parent is the chance to right the wrongs from your childhood. "You spend 18 years in your parents' home, so their ways become normal for you," Dunning says. "But if it doesn't feel right, you can make new rules." You can also go overboard compensating for your parents' missteps, however. To tap into whether your style is working, ask yourself, *Are my kids responding to me the way I want?* If not, examine your choices in certain situations and tweak them to meet your kids' needs *and* your own.

3. **CELEBRATE YOUR STYLE.** It's not often that your kids will tell you what a great job you're doing at being their mom. Borba recommends recording your parenting triumphs and wisdom in a log. You might write, "When I lower my voice, it diffuses Will's tantrums." Says Borba, "It gives you confidence because you're not only tracking successes but also making an effort to improve—and both are signs of a good parent." Add to this journal the

When You Realize Your Child Is Growing Up

"When my kids were little, I focused on establishing their routines, dressing them up in cute outfits, and buying the latest toys. Motherhood was new and exciting, and I felt like I was playing house. Then, about a month ago, I basically freaked out when my 8-year-old was getting dressed and I realized her body was already starting to change. I thought, I really am a mom—I'm the one responsible for teaching her about her body and periods and all those changes. Ever since then, I've seen my job as a parent in a whole new light—and it scares me. But I'm up for it."

compliments from teachers and other parents that have made you feel good about your parenting style. Don't forget to also record the delicious things your child tells you, like "Mommy, I love you the best."

4. **UNDERSTAND THAT YOUR KID IS UNIQUE.** Kids are not robots that you can program. "Children are born with different temperaments that determine how easy or challenging they're going to be to parent," says psychologist Howard Paul, Ph.D., a professor of clinical psychiatry at the University of Medicine and Dentistry of New Jersey. And since the supreme skill of good parenting is meeting your child's specific needs, no one is better equipped than you are—whatever your style—to parent your child. And remember that parenting is always a give-and-take proposition. Researchers have discovered that even in the newborn period, the baby likely has more impact on Mom than they once thought. Apparently, infants—by communicating through cries and other signals—influence not only Mom's actions (getting her to change a diaper, for example) but also her brain, actually stimulating new neurons, enhancing existing ones, and prepping her to become the particular kind of parent that child will need.

5. **FOLLOW YOUR INSTINCTS.** Nobody knows your child better than you do—not your pediatrician, your neighbor, your mother-in-law, or some guru on TV. "We devalue ourselves as moms when we don't trust our instincts—that mommy-vision you get when your baby is born," Borba says. "Your gut instinct, which is where your parenting style is formed, is almost always right for your child." And when you start listening to your heart, you'll make peace with your parenting style.

You're not overly sensitive: It turns out that your mother *does* think she was a better parent than you are! Two thirds of women ages 50 to 64 say today's mothers are doing a worse job as parents than mothers of their generation did, according to a 2007 survey by the Pew Research Center. Hey, we bet their mothers said the same thing about them, so do your best to tune out the nitpicking, keep up the good work—and promise yourself that you'll never criticize your own daughter's parenting skills.

In Praise of Imperfect Moms

Mention made-from-scratch birthday cakes or online message boards filled with posts from competitive, self-sacrificing moms, and René Syler just shakes her head and laughs. Syler, who was co-anchor of CBS's *The Early Show* and is now an ambassador for Susan G. Komen for the Cure, is at the forefront of a new generation of parents who are saying, "You're still a great mom if you serve takeout for dinner!" The proudly imperfect mom of two talks about the bumps along the road of parenthood that inspired her book, *Good Enough Mother*.

- **TRUST YOUR GUT.** I feel like today we are in "mommy do-right" overload. It's that competitiveness that I rail against. You don't have to read books about how to be a good mom or worry about what your neighbors will think. You spend more time with your children than anyone, and you instinctively know what's right for them.

- **TAKE A TIME OUT.** It's okay to put yourself first and to say, "I need a break." To be a good mom, I need to be a well-rounded person. And that means having adult conversations and having friends and interests apart from the kids. And they have interests apart from mine, too. So when we're together, we have more to share with each other.

Am I a Good Enough Mom?

Have you been on the receiving end of meddlesome opinions, disapproving glares, and outright countermands from the Parenting Peanut Gallery: the folks in your life who sit on the sidelines and heckle you with child-rearing judgments—or, even worse, flout your mom rules and policies behind your back—with no regard for your feelings or authority?

While these digs don't leave visible scarring, they can undercut your natural mothering instincts and leave you plain old fighting mad. "There is no shortage of people ready to pick apart your parenting skills," says parenting expert Michele Borba. "It can be hurtful, but when you let them shake your confidence in who you are as a mom, that's when the real damage is done."

The secret to being a great mother is believing in yourself. And one of the best ways to do that is to silence that Parenting Peanut Gallery, once and for all. Here's how:

- **STAND UP FOR YOURSELF.** Address criticism as soon as it happens, so you don't hold in your anger and let it fester. "We women spend a lot of time questioning whether something should or shouldn't make us angry instead of confronting our true feelings," says Borba. "Don't be rude, but let a criticizer know they've crossed a line." Not so quick with a comeback? Bria Simpson, author of *The Balanced Mom: Raising Your Kids Without Losing Yourself*, suggests using this easy script: "I know you have different ideas about parenting. I respect yours and I need you to respect mine."

- **USE AMMO FROM THE EXPERTS.** Your instincts are your best handbook to mothering. But it doesn't hurt to arm yourself with informed guidance. Read a book or two—but not 20. Consult your pediatrician. Talk to friends whose parenting styles you admire. "Mix and match to arrive at your own style," says Debbie Glasser, Ph.D., founder of NewsForParents.org. "When you find out what works for you, you won't be so vulnerable to the push and pull of outsiders."

And when you really want to get the quibblers off your back, never underestimate the power of these three words: "My pediatrician says…" With that preface you get instant cred, even if you say that your baby is allergic to mauve. Seriously.

● **GET YOUR GUY ON YOUR SIDE.** "Spousal sabotage is a big complaint from moms—who often play 'bad cop' by default when dads just want to have fun," says Simpson. Avoid chastising your partner in front of the kids in the heat of the moment. "That kind of squabbling undermines both parents' authority and teaches kids to play you against each other," she explains. Instead, pull your guy aside and quietly explain that his actions undercut your efforts. Then suggest alternatives to his rowdy behavior, such as reading a book with the children or participating in what you're doing so he's not sabotaging you. Later, follow up with him—make sure you're still on the same page about house rules and remind him how crucial it is that you maintain a united parenting front.

Meanwhile, it's also critical to remain somewhat flexible—especially when your kids are at a friend's or relative's house. "When you model flexibility, children learn positive lessons about problem-solving," says Elizabeth Berger, M.D., a child psychiatrist and the author of *Raising Kids with Character*.

● **DITCH THE PEOPLE WHO BRING YOU DOWN.** Feeling a certain amount of self-doubt about our mothering is normal, says Borba. But when your friends actually add to your parenting insecurity, it might be time to find a new mommy group. For Patty Kamson, 44, a nearly 20-year friendship had to end because her pal kept criticizing her parenting skills. "She thought I was soft on my kids and had no qualms voicing her opinion," says Patty, who lives in Los Angeles. While the criticisms never led Patty to change her mothering style, there were times when I wondered, *What if she's right?*, she says. But when Patty's daughter had a meltdown during a get-together, her now former friend "began to lay into me about how my kids and I need to toughen up," she says. So Patty cut her loose. "Riding you about how you mother? Nothing cuts deeper than that," she explains. "I feel better about my parenting—and myself—without that toxic relationship."

- **STAY TRUE TO YOU.** All mommy, all the time, isn't good for your kids, and it isn't good for you either. To keep your own inner voice from being drowned out by the cacophony from underminers, you have to stay connected to the woman you were before you became a mom. Taking just 15 minutes a day for yourself for some quiet reflection will help you hone and trust your instincts. "You're much less affected by what others say if you trust your own gut," says Simpson. And while you'll never be totally free of folks who carp about your parenting choices, the only critic who really matters is the one you tuck in at night.

What Moms Teach Moms

Women who grew up with mothers who enjoyed being a parent are more likely to feel satisfied with their lives—and their identity as a mother—than women who felt that their moms were unhappy in their mother role, according to a study from New York University (NYU). In fact, though many factors come into play in predicting a mom's happiness—including relationships with spouses, work, and child care—the mother-daughter bond seems especially important. "If your mother did not enjoy being a mother, you will probably feel unsettled as a parent because you mirror her feelings whether you're aware of it or not," says Jennifer Stuart, Ph.D., a clinical psychologist at NYU Medical Center and author of the study. So are you doomed if you feel you missed out on good mothering? "As an adult, you get to make up for what went wrong in your own childhood," says Stuart. "Just understanding how your relationship with your own mother affects your satisfaction as a parent—along with choosing other maternal role models—can make you a less resentful and happier mom."

What Kids Teach Moms

We teach our kids everything from language to how to dress themselves. And they're teaching us too. Can you add to the list of important life lessons that we learn from our kids?

What Our Children Can Teach Us about Happiness

When it comes to following your bliss, kids have the art down pat. Here, moms share the make-you-smile secrets they've learned from their little ones.

Appreciate small things.

"One day, on my way home from a run of errands gone bad, I swung by to pick up my son, Nate, then 8, who'd been playing at a friend's house. While he chattered about the fun he'd had, my mind churned through all I'd failed to get done. 'Will Dad be home for dinner?' he asked. 'Think so,' I said. 'Great! What are we having?' he asked. Good question. 'Uh, how about macaroni and cheese?' I replied. A deep sigh of contentment came from the backseat. 'I love my life,' Nate said. His words were like a mood defibrillator. My son's simple satisfaction lifted me straight out of my autopilot loop of worry and let me see my life with fresh appreciation: I was driving down a beautiful mountain road on a glorious summer's day with my wonderful son, with the prospect of a cozy family dinner at home—I loved my life, too!"

Choose your mood.

"When my daughter, Jessica, was a preschooler, she was learning all about choices—you can have a cookie or a scoop of ice cream, but not both; you can wear the green sweater or the blue one, but not both. She was also learning about emotions, and she'd ask, 'Is Mama happy? Is Mama sad? Is Mama mad?' One especially trying day, after I'd yelled a lot, she asked, 'Is Mama mad?' I told her 'No, Mama's not mad anymore.' And she said, 'Mama picked happy!' She was right! I was struggling very hard to calm down, so I was choosing to be happy. Now every time I veer toward a rotten mood, I try to remember I can 'pick happy.'"

Love generously.

"My son, Jonathan, 6, is constantly teaching me how to express love—with passion, creativity, and volume. In the supermarket, he'll shout, 'Mom, I love you more than all the blades of sand on the beach!' and plant a kiss on my cheek. While watching TV, he'll squeeze his baby sister and declare, 'You are so cute I can't stand it!' He shows me that the path to happiness is appreciating those you love and telling them so as often as you can."

Skip a little.

"When my daughter, Deanna, was 5, she skipped everywhere. It didn't matter what the occasion—holidays, parties, going to the store—she skipped. When I asked her why, she told me skipping made her happy. 'You can't be mad and skipping, Mom,' she said. And it's true! So we skip—I skip, she skips, even my husband skips."

Turn to-do's into to-enjoys.

"One fall, my then 1½-year-old son, Brent, and I were raking leaves in our yard. As he played nearby, I was overexerting myself and practically cursing all the trees for having made such a mess. Then I looked over at my son. He was in an area I hadn't raked yet, stepping on the dry leaves to hear the crackling noise they made, and smiling happily. He taught me that some chores are pleasures if you choose to look at them that way."

Redefine success.

"One day, my 4-year-old, Megan, went with me to the post office to mail orders for my online retail business. I was wishing I had 77 orders to mail rather than a paltry seven. Meanwhile, Megan was excitedly counting the orders into the drop box, exclaiming, 'Mommy! There are seven new people who are going to love your work!' She reminded me to take pleasure in what I had accomplished instead of being disappointed by what I hadn't."

Recapture your childhood bliss.

"While swinging one day, my son, James, 3, closed his eyes and stretched out his arms as the wind blew through his hair. He had the most delightful smile—one of pure pleasure—the kind you only see on a child's face. I decided to swing next to him, closing my eyes and letting my senses guide me, just like he did. I heard the wind in my ears and felt the rhythm of swinging. In that moment I experienced complete freedom and sheer pleasure."

Go on impulse.

"When my daughter was 2, she was helping me 'fold' the laundry when she suddenly stripped off her nightgown, put on a pair of her daddy's clean undies (which came up to her armpits), and started dancing. It made me realize that I need to cut loose and enjoy myself more—not wearing my hubby's underpants, but in other ways."

Be a best friend.

"My daughter's best friend got home from school early one day and called with big news. Both she and my 6-year-old daughter had lost a tooth on the same day, at the very same hour! I learn so much about happiness from watching my daughter with her friend—seeing the way they care for each other, copy each other, sing together, even fight and make up. They remind me of how much I love my best friend, Laura, and to always take good care of our friendship."

Spread joy—insist on it!

"My toddler is so crazy about carrots that he often has one in each hand all day long. Once, he really wanted me to have some, and with sticky fingers covered in yogurt, he shoved his carrot in my mouth. He was so happy that he squealed, 'Bah!' at the top of his lungs when I took a bite. It was a reminder of the happiness that comes from sharing something we love with others."

Pursue your passion.

"Nicholas, my 9-year-old son, is quite the artist. He needs to draw every day. I still remember how a few nights before he started kindergarten, he came downstairs way past his bedtime, paper in hand, exhausted. He said, 'I'm really tired, but I just have to color!' His passion for art reminds me how happy I am to be a writer, and I think of what he said whenever I get a rejection letter."

Savor joy while it lasts.

"My 3-year-old son, Nate, loves cars. On one car ride, he was taking in the view of zillions of cars on the Ben Franklin Bridge when, to his delight, a big purple bus painted all over in ads rolled by. He took it all in with great glee. Then he raised a hand, said, 'Bye-bye!' and turned his head and fell asleep. Nate's happiness lesson: Don't cling to moments of perfect joy, just relish them and have faith that more will come."

Surprise! Kids Make You Eat Better

You may feel like you'll never get your pre-baby figure back, but chances are you're living healthier than ever: The proportion of women who get three or more servings of fruits and vegetables *and* eat breakfast every day is much higher 2 years postpartum than prior to pregnancy, says a study in the *Journal of Nutrition Education and Behavior.*

CHAPTER TWO

Eat, Drink, and Be Healthy

Junk food is out, veggies are in—you already know the basics of eating right. But do you know *why* eating dinner together as a family is so important—and how to make it happen in today's hectic world? Can you identify a food allergy—and work around it? Do you know the advantages—and disadvantages—of drinking milk? Can you boost your child's body image, especially when it relates to food? The answers are incredibly important, and they're all here.

Eating Right

Getting kids to eat isn't usually a problem, but getting them to eat healthful, nutritious foods can often turn into a battle of wills. These tips will turn your troops into happy, healthy eaters, and earn you a medal of honor.

5 Easy Ways to Get Your Kids to Eat Healthier

It's no secret that a healthy diet helps kids grow strong and improves their mood and brain function. But how do you actually get kids to eat well? Think small. "You can make little changes to how, what, and when your child eats for big nutritional payoffs," says a pediatric dietitian Marilyn Tanner-Blasiar, a spokesperson for the American Dietetic Association. Here's what to do:

1. **REEL THEM IN WITH FISH NUGGETS.** Replace the chicken in nuggets with fish and your child gets omega-3 fatty acids, which feed the brain and prevent plaque buildup in the arteries. To make fish nuggets (most frozen fish sticks have unhealthy trans fats), cut up a mild fish fillet such as cod or flounder, roll it in bread crumbs, spray with olive oil, and bake for 10 minutes at 375 degrees. Don't use shark, king mackerel, swordfish, or tilefish—the mercury in these can harm the brain and nervous system.

2. **DITCH THE WHOLE MILK FOR SKIM.** Just three glasses of whole milk a day give kids 4 and older 75 percent of their recommended daily maximum of artery-blocking saturated fat—and that's in addition to the saturated fat they get from butter, cheese, and meat. Between ages 1 and 2, when kids are growing

Real Advice from Real Moms

How Do You Get Your Kid to Sit Still Longer Than 30 Seconds at the Dinner Table?

"Our family made a rule that whenever Jake, 5, stood up, someone else at the table would be allowed to take a bite of Jake's dessert at the end of the meal, and we kept track with a crayon on his kid's menu. When he saw everyone else getting bites of his ice cream, he got mad! We only had to do it a couple of times before he learned his lesson."

"Everyone at our table gets at least 5 minutes to talk about their day. The kids know they will have this chance, and they wait for it anxiously without getting up. In our family, once conversation starts going, it's hard to stop it!"

"Our 7-year-old son Caleb's preferred method of sitting is on his head. So when we sit down, I tell him that there is glue on his tushy, and he is stuck in place. If he starts to squirm and tries to do a headstand, I yell in mock horror, 'Oh, no, you're getting glue in your hair!'"

by leaps and bounds, whole milk is recommended. But older kids should switch to a lower-fat milk. Start with 2 percent, then give her 1 percent, then try skim. If your child just won't drink the lower-fat milks, go back to whole, but cut out butter or choose lower-fat cheeses and meats.

3. **THINK FRUIT, NOT BUTTER, FOR BAKING.** Instead of buying cakes and cookies—most of which contain more artery-clogging fats—bake your own and use applesauce, mashed bananas, or pumpkin puree in place of some or all of the butter or oil. To start, try this healthy dessert recipe from Bethany Thayer, a registered dietitian in Detroit: Take a box of chocolate cake mix, add pumpkin puree instead of oil, mix as instructed, and bake in a mini-muffin pan. "They taste like chocolate brownies," says Thayer.

4. **CHOOSE WHOLE WHEAT OVER WHITE.** White bread and pasta are "stripped of fiber and nutrients," says Thayer. A better option: whole wheat, which retains the fiber and nutrients of the grain. Buy products with "whole wheat" listed as one of the first two ingredients ("enriched wheat flour" doesn't cut it). With bread, cut off the crust—it's not any more nutritious than the rest, and its texture can turn kids off. Wheat pastas can be gritty, so start with the thin kinds, such as angel hair.

5. **SERVE VEGGIES—AS SOUP.** "Kids' aversion to vegetables sometimes has to do with texture," says Thayer. Her advice: Smooth things out by turning veggies into pureed soups. Whip up some beta-carotene-rich squash soup or antioxidant-rich creamed tomato (use low-fat milk). And who knows—maybe when your child realizes that the yummy "green soup" is actually broccoli, he'll be up for eating some "trees" as nature made them.

Ever wonder what happens to that apple or rice cake you pack in your kid's lunch every day? There's a good chance it's winding up somewhere other than her belly. Seventy percent of kids admit that they throw their lunch-box snack away, give it to a friend, or bring it back home, according to a poll of 300 children by Kellogg's. Is it possible to pack a healthy snack your kid will actually eat? Missy Chase Lapine, author of *The Sneaky Chef,* offers up snack ideas that are nutritious *and* irresistible:

- Mix some chocolate chips or M&Ms with nuts and dried blueberries or cranberries for a delicious trail mix.
- Freeze a yogurt tube. Bonus: It acts as an ice pack and keeps the rest of the lunch cool.
- Put apple slices or dried apricots in a baggie with a small plastic container of chocolate sauce for dipping.

How the Experts Get Their Kids to Eat Healthy

What? You thought nutritionists' kids were *born* with a taste for spinach? As if! Learn their parents' tricks here.

Play with their food.

"I'll admit, it's tough to get my kids to eat vegetables. But I know that kids eat with their eyes, so if I can make it fun, they won't notice they're eating healthily. The other day I put a scoop of tuna salad in the middle of cut-up bell pepper slices, so it looked like a flower—my kids loved it. I'll also make smiley faces with peas or a funny face with carrots."

DAVID GROTTO, R.D.
AUTHOR OF *101 FOODS THAT COULD SAVE YOUR LIFE,*
AND DAD OF THREE

Real Advice from Real Moms

How Do You Get Your Kid to Sit Still Longer Than 30 Seconds at the Dinner Table?

"We play a game: Someone picks a category, like animals or fruits, and then we go around the table with everyone taking a bite of their food and then naming something in that category until we run out of items. This can go on for a long time, and, weirdly, it really works!"

Add texture and taste to their meals.

"My daughter loves when I make my healthy pancakes for her on the weekends. I use a whole-wheat mix and add an egg for extra protein. Then I top them with banana slices and peanut butter. I serve the pancakes with a glass of foamy nonfat milk that I make with a milk frother. It's more fun to drink than plain milk."

LOLA O'ROURKE, R.D.
SPOKESPERSON FOR THE ADA IN SEATTLE,
AND MOM OF ONE

Teach them how food works.

"From the time my daughter was a baby, we talked about the special things different foods do for her body. She boasts how milk helps her teeth and bones stay strong, how carrots and corn help her eyes, and how nuts keep her skin healthy. Now when we introduce her to new foods, the first question out of her mouth is, 'Mom, what does this help my body do?' And that gets her excited to try it."

SUSAN KUNDRAT, R.D.
PRESIDENT AND FOUNDER OF NUTRITION ON THE MOVE
IN URBANA, IL, AND MOM OF ONE

Let them customize their order.

"When I make omelets, I first arrange low-fat cheese, ham, tomatoes, bell peppers, mushrooms, and onions into little bowls. As I'm cooking, I let my older son throw in any and all of the ingredients he wants. When he feels he's taken part in making a meal, he eats more."

LAUREN SLAYTON, R.D.
OWNER OF FOODTRAINERS, A NUTRITION COUNSELING CENTER
IN NEW YORK CITY, AND MOM OF TWO

EAT, DRINK, AND BE HEALTHY

Make your own "fast food."

"On Sundays, I make a big batch of healthy chicken nuggets. Then I freeze them and they're ready fast during the week. When I add some baked french fries and some nutritious dips like yogurt sauce or salsa, my son is in fast-food heaven."

PHILIP GOGLIA, PH.D.
FOUNDER OF THE NUTRITION AND FITNESS CLINIC G SYSTEMS CONCEPTS IN
LOS ANGELES, AND DAD OF ONE

Introduce the food groups.

"At each meal, my kids know they have to have at least one option from each of the four food groups, and they can choose which. So for lunch, they may have a sandwich made on something from the grain group, like whole-wheat bread or a pita, with something from the protein group (turkey, peanut butter, or tuna). They also have a choice of a favorite fruit or vegetable, like lettuce and tomato on the sandwich, or carrots, celery, a peach, or an apple on the side. Finally, they can choose between a glass of low-fat milk or yogurt from the dairy group."

JEANNIE GAZZANIGA MOLOO, PH.D.
A NUTRITIONIST IN PRIVATE PRACTICE IN ROSEVILLE, CA,
AND MOM OF THREE

Serve a snack before supper.

"Before dinner, I often serve an appetizer—a big platter of fresh, colorful veggies, like carrots, cucumbers, zucchini, and red and yellow bell peppers, with a tasty dip like hummus, mustard, or balsamic vinegar. Children are typically very hungry before dinner, so it's a great time to get in their vegetables."

ANN G. KULZE, M.D.
FOUNDER OF JUST WELLNESS, LLC,
IN CHARLESTON, SC, AND MOM OF FOUR

Real Advice from Real Moms

Win the Sweets War

"I serve my kids whatever I plan to feed them for dinner, including a small portion of dessert, all together on those plastic sectioned character plates (Dora the Explorer and SpongeBob are their favorites). Each area has chicken, rice, salad, and a Popsicle, or something similar. I don't bug them to eat the veggies before the treat, so even if they have dessert first, it's small enough that they don't fill up—therefore they always move on to eat a nice amount of dinner. It works like a charm."

Let them eat pizza—even for breakfast.

"My 11-year-old isn't a big breakfast eater—she doesn't even like sugary cereal, pancakes, or waffles. But I know how important it is to eat in the morning—blood sugar is the brain's main source of fuel, and after an overnight fast it's low, which can cause distraction and lead to a lack of concentration in school. So if she wants to have a slice of pizza, a peanut butter and jelly sandwich, or even macaroni and cheese in the morning, that's fine by me."

KRISTIN REIMERS, R.D.
ASSOCIATE DIRECTOR OF THE INTERNATIONAL CENTER
FOR SPORTS NUTRITION IN OMAHA, AND MOM OF TWO

Hide the healthy stuff.

"Even though my son won't eat vegetables, he gobbles up my spinach patties. That's because I conceal the spinach in something he likes—the patty, which I serve as a side dish. My other tricks: When I make tomato sauce, I throw in peas, and I add carrots and spinach to white rice. If vegetables are buried in something he likes, he's more willing to accept them."

ANDREA SCHAEFFER, R.D.
A NUTRITIONIST AT MEMORIAL SLOAN-KETTERING
CANCER CENTER IN NEW YORK CITY, AND MOM OF TWO

Say okay to snacks.

"There are so many teenage girls with eating issues, so my goal is to not make food a big deal. Instead of saying no, I offer choices. When my preschooler asks if she can have a piece of candy, I always say, 'Sure, you can, or you can have some strawberries in your Strawberry Shortcake bowl.' More often than not, she'll pick the strawberries."

SHALENE MCNEILL, PH.D.
A NUTRITIONIST IN THE SAN ANTONIO AREA,
AND MOM OF ONE

It's Dinnertime!

Rounding up the troops for dinner each day is a logistical challenge for every parent. But a family sit-down brings more than just a healthy meal to the table. "Eating dinner together sets the stage for positive family interactions, makes kids feel more secure about themselves, encourages good nutrition, and lowers the risk of eating disorders and obesity," asserts Miriam Weinstein, author of *The Surprising Power of Family Meals.* And kids who have frequent family dinners are less likely to try drugs, drink, or smoke, and they're also more likely to get better grades, according to the National Center on Addiction and Substance Abuse at Columbia University. That's great news, but all the research in the world won't make family dinner happen. What will? Start with these mom-tested strategies to get your family back to the dinner table.

- **MAKE DINNER A MOVABLE FEAST.** When Dad has to stay late at the office, or they're busy with an activity, the Kiner family of Phoenix doesn't give up on their family dinner plans. "When Dad's working late, sometimes we'll meet him somewhere on the way home from work and have a special meal out, explains Anne Kiner, mom of two, ages 10 and 7. "The kids love it because it's a chance to try different food than what they normally have at home. Plus, we all get to eat together."

- **THINK OUTSIDE THE DINNER HOUR.** Can't pin everyone down for a weeknight dinner? Turn lunch into a family affair instead. If lunch isn't possible, either, set aside weekend family meal times.

Real Advice from Real Moms

Dinner in a Hurry

NOODLE NOSH
"My kids love noodles, so I usually boil some ahead of time to keep in the fridge. I just melt cheese over them in the microwave or make a cold pasta salad."

AT-HOME SALAD BAR
"We buy bagged salad, and I set out bowls of different toppings on a large wooden Lazy Susan that I keep in the middle of the table. This way, we can spin it around and everyone can easily reach. Ditto with plain baked potatoes!"

INSTANT ASIAN
"One thing I always have up my domestic sleeve is Hibachi House—totally yummy frozen microwavable Asian dinners. I kid you not, I can have it on the table in less time than it takes to find the phone number and place an order at my local teriyaki takeout place."

QUICKIE PIZZAS
"Our favorite 10-minute meal is Boboli pizza crust, bagels, or English muffins topped with tomato sauce and shredded mozzarella cheese and then popped in the toaster oven for a few minutes."

- **DITCH THE DINNER TABLE.** Consider having an indoor picnic to conjure up some cozy family togetherness. "Every once in a while we take out a tablecloth and eat right on the living room floor!" says Shana Less of Hoboken, NJ.

- **LET ONE PARENT DO DINNER DUTY.** Have supper as a family even if one parent isn't able to make it, recommends Weinstein. This way eating together is more likely to become a regular occurrence, she explains.

- **INTRODUCE A BEFORE-BED SNACK.** It's fine to push dinner later once in a while for older kids. But as Vanessa Monticelli of Union City, NJ, knows, younger kids just can't last that long. Her solution? "On the nights my husband works late, I'll usually feed our son, age 2, his dinner around 5:30 or 6 P.M.," she says. "Then when Dad gets home around 7, we all sit down together and our son eats fruit or dessert while we eat dinner and catch up on the day's events."

- **COUNT YOUR BLESSINGS.** "We begin each meal with everyone saying three thankful things," says Julia McGill of Keswick, VA. "It changes our focus from whatever negativity the day has brought, such as conflicts with peers or bosses, to the positive things that happen in our lives."

- **GET THE GROUP TALKING.** Try dinnertime games sure to get tongues wagging: FamilyTimeFun Dinner Games & Activities (ftfgames.com), TableTopics Family Edition (tabletopics. com), or a simple "conversation jar" filled with slips of paper that are scribbled with fun, open-ended, imagination-provoking questions (such as "If you could have one magic power, what would it be and why?") that each family member takes a turn to answer.

- **LET THE KIDS HELP OUT.** About once a week the Knoll family of Minneapolis has "Kids Cook Night." Mom Michelle helps her three boys, all under 6, decide what to make by throwing out suggestions and letting them look through recipe books. "I let the boys do as much as they can, but I handle any cutting, the stove, oven, or other potential hazards," says Michelle. "They take pride in the job and love to tell their dad how hard they worked preparing and cooking dinner for the family."
- **MAKE THE MEAL A SPECIAL OCCASION.** "A fun—and educational—ritual we do once a week is to have 'Polite Night,'" says Gretchen Rubin of New York City, mom of two daughters, ages 8 and 2. "Instead of eating casually in the kitchen, we set the dining room table with place mats, cloth napkins, and if I'm being ambitious, a candle. We all practice our best manners—no elbows, no using fingers, no reaching, and napkin in lap."
- **HAVE "JUST-BECAUSE" CELEBRATIONS.** "Sometimes we turn the dinner hour into little parties to celebrate random things, like the first day of summer or the dog's birthday," reveals Kara Paul of Hackettstown, NJ. "The girls [ages 9 and 4] make decorations, and I set out a buffet of hors d'oeuvres for dinner (kid-friendly things, like shrimp cocktail, crudités and dip, cheese and crackers, and deviled eggs). We fix fancy drinks, turn on the music, and have a great time."

So . . . What's for Dinner?

At some point when your child is 3 or 4, it hits you: I have to cook dinner for this kid every night for the next 15 *years*? When you're absolutely stumped for fresh ideas, one of these delicious sites could just be your meal ticket.

Real Advice from Real Moms

Dinner in a Hurry (*continued*)

SIMPLY SANDWICHES
"Our standby dinner is peanut butter sandwiches with carrots and apple slices on the side. As unimaginative as that is, we always have the ingredients, and no one ever seems to tire of that combo."

EGGS ANY WAY
"Nothing cooks faster than eggs—and they go with just about anything you happen to have in the fridge. I make fried-egg sandwiches with cheese, and ham if I have it; scrambled egg burritos with cheese and salsa; or omelets filled with whatever I have—cheese, mushrooms, olives."

It takes about 12 tries before a child starts to like a new food. So don't give up on the broccoli yet!

- **MAKE-YOUR-OWN-DAMN-DINNER.BLOGSPOT.COM:** The creator of this blog, a mom of two in Texas, was tired of cooking separate meals for her husband and kids every night, so she decided to put her 10- and 8-year-olds in charge of their own, uh, darn dinner. (One rule: The meal has to include a protein and a vegetable.) Now her site has become a great source of simple-yet-inspired dinner ideas, like cinnamon chicken with couscous, and barbecued shrimp with grilled apricots.

- **SMITTENKITCHEN.COM:** Written by an amateur chef named Deb, Smitten Kitchen features mouthwatering photos and descriptions, as well as wry commentary about trying to cook in a tiny city apartment. The site features dishes like delicious lemon-ricotta pancakes and savory soups.

- **SPATULATTA.COM:** An award-wining Web site (and book) featuring junior chefs Belle and Liv, ages 11 and 9, Spatulatta goes beyond the usual "kids in the kitchen" pizza-bagel recipes. Streaming videos show how kids can whip up sushi or spinach pie. Mom's Corner gives great tips, such as: Always buy extra ingredients in case the first batch winds up on the floor.

Food Allergies

Food allergies can be frightening, especially when you feel like you have no control over them—but you do. Here's how to reassert control.

Worried About Food Allergies?

Yes, they're on the rise. But you can manage the symptoms, and maybe even keep kids from getting allergies in the first place.

An increasing number of children have allergies to everyday foods such as milk, eggs, peanuts, and fish. The prevalence of seasonal and other respiratory allergies also appears to be on the rise. Experts aren't entirely sure why allergy rates have skyrocketed, but one of the most popular theories—called the "hygiene hypothesis"—focuses on a lack of early exposure to germs. Decreased exposure to germs may lessen your kid's ability to fight them. (And remember that soap and water are equally as effective as most antibacterial products at fighting germs—without killing the "good," protective bacteria that antibacterial products might.) Genetics also play a role: If you or your husband have allergies, there is a greater chance that your child will have them too. One study showed that 25 percent of infants with a family history of allergies went on to develop them.

Unfortunately, there is no cure for allergies, and food allergies are particularly unpredictable and terrifying for kids and parents. But there are ways to help you recognize, treat—and even prevent—them.

WHAT TO LOOK FOR: Your child may have a food allergy if he has itchy skin, a tingly mouth, rashes, hives, vomiting, stomach pain, and/or diarrhea after

If it isn't clear what's causing your child's symptoms, her doctor may suggest food allergy tests, which will help pinpoint the triggers so you can eliminate them from her diet. These tests can be performed at any age by an allergist or by your pediatrician. The two most common types can also be used to determine whether a child has outgrown a food allergy:

- **SKIN-PRICK TEST:** This test involves placing a small amount of a suspected allergen on your child's skin through a prick or scratch on the back or forearm. A small red lump similar to a mosquito bite will form within 15 to 20 minutes if the test is positive. Skin tests are usually done because they're rapid, reliable, and cost less than blood tests.

- **BLOOD TEST:** Less sensitive than a skin test, blood tests are most commonly used to monitor an allergy over time. Blood tests are also helpful if a child is on antihistamines, since the drugs won't affect the result (as they will with skin tests).

eating. The most common food allergies are to milk, eggs, wheat, soy, peanuts, tree nuts, fish, and shellfish. They account for 90 percent of food allergy reactions. (Food allergies shouldn't be confused with food intolerances or sensitivities, which can cause digestive symptoms similar to those associated with allergies, but don't provoke the immune system response that causes hives, rash, and difficulty breathing. Children with food intolerances often can handle small amounts of the offending food without symptoms.) If left untreated, food allergies can lead to poor growth, life-threatening symptoms such as difficulty breathing and bodily swelling, and even death.

THE ACTION PLAN: You can reduce your child's risk of allergies as early as infancy. Studies suggest that exclusively breast-feeding babies for at least 4 months may help prevent or delay a cow's milk allergy. If you can't breast-feed, or you plan to supplement breast milk with formula, ask your doctor about hydrolyzed formula. And while it's long been recommended that parents delay a child's exposure to certain foods such as milk, eggs, and nuts, the American Academy of Pediatrics now states that there are insufficient data to support these guidelines. When your baby starts eating solids, introduce foods one at a time and watch her after she eats. Food allergy reactions usually appear within minutes, but can sometimes take several hours to show up. If you suspect an allergy, keep a diary of everything your child eats and any symptoms. If you're unsure which foods are causing a reaction, your doctor may help pinpoint them by having you eliminate certain foods and then, under his supervision, reintroduce them to watch for symptoms. He may also refer you to an allergist (see "Allergy Testing 101," page 51).

ADDRESS THE ALLERGY: If your child is diagnosed with an allergy, pay close attention to food packaging. The FDA requires that labels clearly state whether a food contains any of the top eight food allergens listed above. If an ingredient list isn't provided, call the manufacturer or simply don't use the product. Make sure other parents, teachers, and caregivers know what to do in case of a reaction. And talk to your kid about how to handle one when you're not there. Your child's doctor may suggest she carry an EpiPen. As your child gets older, you may be able to gradually reintroduce offending foods, but check with her doctor first. The good news is, about 80 percent to 90 percent of egg, milk, wheat, and soy allergies vanish by age 5. Only 20 percent of children outgrow peanut allergies, though, and fewer outgrow allergies to tree nuts and seafood.

Juice, Milk, and More

The importance of having your child drink enough—and of the proper liquids—gets overshadowed by the importance of eating right. But drinking right is important too, and it's different for different age ranges. Here's why, and what to do about it.

Is Your Child Drinking Enough?

As a general rule, young children should consume 24 ounces of liquids a day, preferably water, says Adrienne Bean, M.D., a pediatrician in southern California. Skip caffeinated beverages, and go easy on sugary drinks—both can be dehydrating. Your child will urinate every 2 to 3 hours if he's well hydrated. If he's dizzy or his skin is flushed but dry, he's not drinking enough. Keep the liquid flowing, Bean says. "When kids complain of thirst, they're *already* dehydrated."

The Skinny on Juice

Juice has gotten a bad rap for contributing to the increase in childhood obesity. That is, until now. You can give your kid back his juice box, thanks to a study from Baylor College of Medicine that found 100 percent fruit juice actually *doesn't* cause weight gain in preschoolers. "One hundred percent fruit juice provides valuable nutrients such as vitamin C, potassium, and magnesium that aren't found in other fruit drinks," says Theresa Nicklas, Ph.D., the lead researcher on the study. Read the label and make sure it's really 100 percent fruit juice—otherwise, it's not much better for your kid than candy, she says. Aim for no more than 6 ounces of juice per day. And, to give your child the most nutrients, opt for orange juice: It contains twice as much magnesium and potassium and three times as much folate as apple or grape juice.

How Much Milk is Enough?

The recommended three 8-ounce servings a day is plenty. And children ages 9 to 14 who drank more than that were 25 percent more likely to become overweight than kids who stuck to the three-servings rule, according to a study in the journal *Archives of Pediatrics & Adolescent Medicine*. The big surprise: Skim and low-fat milk were associated with *more* weight gain, possibly because parents allow kids to overindulge when it's low-fat. The bottom line: "If your child is overweight, even a 'healthy' food has calories and needs to be counted," says Helaine Rockett, coauthor of the study and a senior health analyst at Massachusetts General Hospital in Boston.

Got Milk?

On hot days, kids love to cool off with "bug juice," water, and ice pops—which may be why kids drink less milk during July and August, according to a national survey on children's beverage consumption. Sneak some bone-building calcium back into their diet with one of these ideas from registered dietitian Amy Jamieson-Petonic, a spokesperson for the American Dietetic Association: Make your own ice pops out of calcium-fortified orange juice, or blend 8 ounces of low-fat milk with a frozen banana and fresh strawberries, kiwis, or raspberries, and a handful of ice cubes for a scrumptious summer smoothie.

Weight

It's all over the news—and in our homes. Our kids are overweight—but why? And what are the first steps to take if we suspect a problem? Find out here.

Why Are Our Kids Overweight?

Within the past 30 years, the rate of childhood obesity has *tripled* among kids ages 6 to 11. Here, some top reasons why—from a report by the Society for Research in Child Development.

- Today's kids are eating more calorie-dense foods (think cupcakes, potato chips, and soda) than ever before.
- The average child sees more than 40,000 TV commercials per year, 32,000 of which are for junk food.
- Kids are more likely to be driven places instead of walking or riding a bike.
- Kids are less active today thanks to increased "screen time," such as watching TV or surfing the Internet.

Would You Know if Your Kid Was Overweight?

Every mom thinks her children are beautiful, but when you look at your child through the haze of mom-colored glasses, you may be missing a crucial red flag: In a study from Deakin University in Australia, 89 percent of parents of overweight 5- and 6-year-olds failed to recognize that their own child had a weight problem. It's easy to attribute this to motherly love—but experts also point to the plumping up of Americans in general. "If your child looks like everyone else, there is no reason for you to think he's overweight," points out Roberta Anding, a registered dietitian and the spokesperson of the American Dietetic Association. But pleasantly plump can easily slide into obesity, which raises your child's risk for diabetes, hypertension, and asthma. Anding suggests taking these steps to keep your child healthy:

- **GET A PROFESSIONAL OPINION.** At your child's next checkup, ask your doctor to calculate his body mass index (BMI)—a ratio of height to weight that gives a good picture of whether your kid is overweight—then discuss if the BMI is in the healthy range. "If he tells you your child is overweight, don't take it personally," says Anding. "Be grateful that you found out so you can do something about it."

- **ELIMINATE SUGARY DRINKS.** Just by clearing soft drinks and Kool-Aid out of the house, you can save your child 500 calories a day, says Anding. "Even if he sometimes eats pizza and fast food, that makes a huge difference."

- **PLAY TOGETHER.** To avoid making your child feel self-conscious about his weight, get the whole family moving, says Anding. "If you all go to the park or play tag in the backyard *together*, it won't feel like hard work or exercise," she says.

6 Ways to Help Your Kid Love His Healthy Body

- **DO** talk up his internal strengths—like sense of humor and enthusiasm—instead. Encourage him in areas he's passionate about, whether it's doing puzzles or caring for the family pet.
- **DON'T** forbid foods.
- **DO** feed the entire family the same food, even if one child is heavier. And if you serve healthy portions of nutritious foods, everyone wins!
- **DON'T** insist your child follow the "clean your plate" rule.
- **DO** respect her inner signals of fullness. She'll learn good portion control and to eat only when she's hungry.
- **DON'T** complain about your body.

Body Image

Anyone who's ever had a kid—in fact, anyone who's ever *been* a kid—knows that how children feel about their bodies shapes how they feel about themselves. Here's what to do if your child is having body doubts.

Boost Your Child's Body Confidence

Concern about body image is an increasingly common one among parents of elementary school-age kids. "Body-image issues used to start at puberty, but we're seeing problems in 5- to 8-year-olds now," says Ira M. Sacker, M.D., a leading expert on eating disorders. Media messages about the "right" body type—unattainable for the vast majority of us—are so pervasive that even younger kids can't escape them.

As the number-one influence in your young child's life, you can shore up her self-love by sending her conscious and explicit positive body messages every chance you get. Here, the most common body doubts kids feel at different stages. When you hear them, challenge them, and give your kids the tools to fight them long-term.

Preschoolers

BODY DOUBT

Your chubby 3-year-old seems shy about wearing her dance leotard for the first time.

HOW TO RESPOND

It's not too early to instill the idea that body image should be based on function instead of appearance. "Rather than saying, 'You look cute in your leotard,' say, 'You look so strong!'" advises Ann Kearney-Cooke, Ph.D., director of the Cincinnati Psychotherapy Institute and author of *Change Your Mind, Change Your Body*. Kids who feel competent have higher self-esteem, so teach your child to ride a bike, swim, and catch a ball.

Kindergartners

BODY DOUBT

Your skinny 5-year-old daughter says, "I hate my soccer shin guards. They make my legs look fat!"

HOW TO RESPOND

Don't dismiss her anxiety—but do question it. "Once children are in school, they hear other kids talking about being fat, and suddenly a child who was happy with her body can become concerned," says Kathy Kater, a psychotherapist in St. Paul and author of *Real Kids Come in All Sizes*. Your instinct may be to say, "Your legs are not fat!" Instead, learn more about what sparked the comment by saying, "That must feel frustrating. Why are you saying that?" It could be she thinks she isn't good at soccer. "Kids often project negative feelings they have about themselves onto their bodies," says Kearney-Cooke. Be empathetic about what's worrying her, but circle back to the body-image message by reminding her of how well her body works. Say, "Your legs run so fast, you need to take care of them."

Early elementary school-age kids

BODY DOUBT

Your chunky 7-year-old son says, "Everyone at school calls me Fatso. I hate being so big!"

HOW TO RESPOND

"Teasing can start at age 7 and becomes even more common by age 8 or 9," says Kater. First, make your child's teacher aware of the situation. Then help your child cope by letting him know that, although too much junk food isn't

How I Learned to Back Off

"When my oldest child was in third grade, he was being picked on. One time, he was invited to a birthday party at a movie theater. I watched children call my son names, and when he sat in the row with other boys, they got up and moved. I asked the boys if they realized how mean they were being and how they would like it if it were happening to them. I also spoke to some of their parents. My son was made fun of even more that year because of what I did, and he resents my actions. I also learned that *he* didn't take their words personally—I did! Now I have learned to let my children have their own lives. If they ask me to step in, I'll be there—but only if they ask."

good for anyone, his basic body type has more to do with genetic roulette. Discuss your family's body type in a matter-of-fact way, saying something like, "Our family tends to have red hair, blue eyes, and a stocky build." At the same time, make eating healthfully easy. Stock the kitchen with nutritious treats (fresh fruit instead of fruity candy) and make sure your child gets exercise every day. If you do that, you'll set him up for physical *and* emotional confidence.

Tweens

BODY DOUBT

Your developing 9-year-old daughter says, "I don't fit into my jeans. Why is my butt getting so big?"

HOW TO RESPOND

The physical changes of puberty can deal a whammy to even the least image-obsessed kids. Girls need to know that it's normal to gain weight, especially around the hips, at the onset of puberty. Say something like, "I know that must feel strange, but if you eat healthy foods and are active, most of that weight is going to get redistributed in the next few years." Remind boys who are slow to grow that everyone develops at different rates, and let them know you always have time to listen to their concerns.

CHAPTER THREE

Health

The best way to stay healthy is to prevent problems from occurring in the first place, so here's preventive advice on germs (are doggy kisses okay?), winter colds (make colorful meals), and more—plus what to do if your child gets sick anyway. Then there's sleep, exercise, symptoms (is that a simple sore throat or a strep throat that demands a doctor's attention?), and medication. And let's not forget about warm-weather worries (what exactly *is* that rash?) and sex (which you may not want to address, but should). Here's what you need to know to protect your family.

Prevention

An ounce of prevention is worth a pound of cure, as the old saying goes—and the saying has been around forever because it's right! Learn to ward off colds and the flu with the tips here, and don't forget to brush up on preventing dental problems, too.

The Real Deal on Germs

Are you stocking up on antibacterial wipes, obsessively scrubbing under your nails, and scrutinizing your friends' personal hygiene habits to protect against germs? You may be going too far: The vast majority of germs are harmless; experts even say they can be helpful. "Exposure to germs is what teaches young immune systems to fend off bad bugs and mature into efficient germ fighters," says Robert Frenck, Jr., M.D., a pediatric infectious disease expert at Cincinnati Children's Medical Center. Keep reading to discover which germ-fighting tactics are time well spent and which ones aren't worth the worry.

Germophobe Rule #1 Public sandboxes are completely off-limits.

REALITY CHECK: Kids may see the playground sandbox as their own private beach, but cats and other critters consider it a public litter box. Although the risk is small, if your child sticks his fingers into his mouth after playing in sand soiled with animal feces, he could get sick with parasites like roundworms, which can lead to fever and stomach pains; or hookworms, which result in painful skin infections and diarrhea. Be sure to wipe his hands with a wet alcohol towelette when he's finished playing, and then wash them again with soap and water when you get home to remove lingering traces of dirt.

Germophobe Rule #2 No doggy kisses allowed.

REALITY CHECK: Unless your child has an open wound that's at risk for infection from germs in the dog's saliva, a canine smooch typically isn't cause for concern, says Frenck. Still, it's best to have your child wash up after he's been slobbered on by any animal. If the dog is unknowingly infected with parasites, they can be found inside its mouth. Besides, you can't be sure what Fido last licked.

Germophobe Rule #3 Fruits and vegetables—even prewashed ones—must be rinsed again at home.

REALITY CHECK: When it comes to food preparation, you can't be too careful. Even prewashed, ready-to-eat foods can be contaminated with traces of dirt, bacteria, and pesticides. To remove these residual contaminants, clean all produce with water and a scrub brush, then pat dry with a clean cloth or paper towel before serving. Remember to wash your hands, utensils, and kitchen surfaces with hot, soapy water after handling fresh produce to avoid contaminating other foods.

Germophobe Rule #4 You wash your child's binkie every time she drops it on the kitchen floor.

REALITY CHECK: Moms joke about the 5-second rule. But any amount of time on the floor is long enough for dropped objects to become contaminated with illness-causing bacteria like salmonella and E. coli, according to a Clemson University study. An object or piece of food dropped on a kitchen or bathroom floor is more likely to pick up these harmful bugs, but it's *always* best to discard dropped food and clean fallen items with hot water and soap before giving them back to your child.

Germophobe Rule #5 Toys are cleaned weekly.

REALITY CHECK: Germs can live on toys for long periods of time, so it's wise to sanitize the items used most often and those that frequently get put in a child's mouth—still, unless a sick child has played with them, a monthly cleaning should suffice. You can safely disinfect many things—from plastic toys to lunch boxes to high chair trays—with a diluted bleach solution. Many plastic toys can be cleaned in the dishwasher. Wash stuffed animals in hot water in the washing machine and dry thoroughly to prevent molding.

Germophobe Rule #6 **Antibacterial products are used throughout your home to keep germs at bay.**

REALITY CHECK: The overuse of antibacterial products has been linked to antibiotic-resistant superbugs, which is one reason the American Medical Association doesn't support their everyday application. Instead, save the heavy-hitting bacteria killers for kitchen and bathroom areas that truly need it, says Elizabeth Scott, Ph.D., codirector of the Center for Hygiene and Health in Home and Community at Simmons College in Boston. And while hand sanitizers work great when you can't get to a sink, soap and water is still best for removing dirt and germs. In fact, according to a recent study, washing for 30 seconds the old-fashioned way kills as much bacteria—90 percent—as most antibacterial products do.

Germophobe Rule #7 **Kids' clothes are always washed separately.**

REALITY CHECK: Once your child is past the newborn stage, when her skin is more sensitive to harsh laundry detergents, there's no reason to create more work for yourself on laundry day—unless someone in your family is sick with a stomach bug, the flu, or a skin infection. "Some bacteria and viruses can survive standard wash cycles," says Harley Rotbart, M.D., author of *Germ Proof Your Kids*. To be safe, wash a sick family member's clothes separately using bleach and the hottest temperature deemed safe for the clothing, and always dry clothes in a hot dryer, which kills more bacteria than air-drying or cool spins. To keep germs from spreading, wash your hands after handling dirty laundry and sanitize your washing machine monthly by running an empty cold-water cycle and adding 1 cup of bleach to the wash water.

Bundling up your kids in hats and scarves in winter will keep them warm and toasty—but it'll also provide a cozy home for lice. Follow our expert tips and you'll be nit-free in no time.

- **PICK THE BEST TREATMENT.** "If your child's hair is fine or easily combed, a nit comb (available over-the-counter at drugstores) works best," says Richard Pollack, Ph.D., an entomologist with the Harvard School of Public Health. For thicker hair, the American Academy of Pediatrics recommends Nix, an over-the-counter chemical rinse.

- **GO GREEN.** There's been a recent push to develop nontoxic lice treatments, thanks in part to lice's growing resistance to the chemicals in products like Nix. One popular treatment: Use Cetaphil Gentle Skin Cleanser to suffocate the lice (for directions go to nuvoforheadlice.com). You can also try coating your child's head with olive oil. Go to the American Head Lice Information Center (Head LicetoDeadLice.com), an organization that advocates nontoxic treatments, for more information.

- **KEEP THE CRITTERS AT BAY.** Lice can't jump or fly, but they can climb. "If you're going to a popular kids' movie, take a rain jacket to throw over the seat's back. Lice can't get up the slick surface," says Joan Sawyer, author of *Head Lice to Dead Lice*. And if there's a lice infestation in your child's class, send your child to school with slightly greasy hair, Sawyer advises—it's harder for lice to attach their eggs.

Easy Ways to Beat Winter Colds

Your child's best defense against bugs and viruses is a good offense. Boost her immune system and she'll be less likely to catch whatever's going around. Here's our expert-devised game plan.

- **FIGHT STRESS WITH *FUN*.** Studies have shown that stress weakens the immune system. And winter "has inherent stressors such as the darkness, the cold, and the fact that kids can't get outside to play as much," says Kathleen Hall, founder of the Stress Institute outside Atlanta. Help your child relieve stress by making him laugh, singing together, or encouraging him to write in a journal. Devise a soothing mantra—like "I am strong"—that he can say if he feels stressed.

- **FOCUS ON FAMILY TIME.** People who are isolated can have weaker immune systems, says Hall. In fact, research has shown that social support enhances your body's defenses against serious illnesses, such as cancer and HIV infection. The same applies to the sniffles—you can help your child dodge a cold simply by spending more time with her. "For children, family is the essential connection for their intimacy needs," says Hall. Make a point to play games, rent movies, or go bowling as a family every week. You'll be building up your child's resistance to illness, and you're having fun together. And that's the cure for whatever ails you.

- **WASH, WASH, AND WASH AGAIN.** One of the reasons kids spread germs so quickly is that they are constantly touching their faces—rubbing their eyes, picking their nose—so whatever germs get on their hands go straight to their eyes, nose, and mouth. Teach them to scrub with soap and warm water after they go to the bathroom, play with communal toys, or play sports, for as long as it takes to sing "Twinkle, Twinkle, Little Star" (about 30 seconds). For those times when she can't find a sink, give her a hand sanitizer. A recent study found that families who used these gels reduced their respiratory infections.

- **KEEP WIPES HANDY.** Yes, germs are *everywhere,* but you don't have to be a hermit to stay healthy. Rotbart suggests you keep a box of antibacterial wipes in your car and have everyone wipe their hands on the way home. "You can't clean the world," he says, "but you can clean yourself after coming into contact with it."

- **BUNDLE UP.** Even though colds and flu are spread by a virus, if you are exposed to that virus while you have a chill, your immune system can't fight it off as well, explains Rotbart. So dress your kids in warm clothes and lined boots on cold days.

- **GET HIM MOVING.** Even if it's freezing outside, bundle up your child and go snowshoeing, ice-skating, or just run around at the playground. "Active kids have better immune function," says David Nieman, a professor of health and exercise science at Appalachian State University in Boone, NC. Plus, regular exercise keeps kids from becoming obese, which Nieman has found to be linked to poor immunity. Stuck indoors? Get your child to bop around to music. "The goal is to log 60 minutes of exercise a day," says Nieman.

- **AVOID GERMY BOOKS.** You know all those dog-eared copies of *Highlights Magazine* in your pediatrician's waiting room? They're covered with the germs of all the sick kids who waited there before you. Instead, bring a book and toys from home to avoid picking up new bugs.

- **MAKE COLORFUL MEALS.** You know that fruit and vegetables are good for your child. But are you giving her enough variety? To ensure that she gets a healthy dose of immune-boosting nutrients (such as the lutein in dark leafy greens, the carotenoids in carrots, and the lycopene in tomatoes), give her fruit and veggies in a rainbow of colors, says Beth Thayer, R.D., a spokesperson for the American Dietetic Association. When you make pizza, top it with tomato sauce and a sprinkle of cheese, broccoli, and orange or yellow peppers.

- **STICK TO HIS BEDTIME.** A good night's rest makes you more resistant to illness, says Jodi Mindell, Ph.D., coauthor of *Take Charge of Your Child's Sleep*. In one study, men who slept more produced more antibodies to a flu vaccine than men who didn't sleep as much. If your child isn't getting enough Zs (infants should get 14 to 15 hours of shut-eye; toddlers,

Beating Winter's Chill

Of course you want your child to be warm when it's cold out. But "parents often pack kids in too much clothing," says Marjorie Hogan, M.D., associate professor of pediatrics at the University of Minnesota Medical School. That could make kids sweaty, and the moisture can make them feel chilly. Here's how to layer up both toddlers and older kids up so they won't overheat.

- Cotton turtleneck
- Fleece pullover
- Sweatpants
- Fleece hat
- Waterproof jacket
- Waterproof, lined mittens that cover wrists
- Boots that cinch at the top to keep snow out

Fight the Flu!

You can't prevent the common cold, but you *can* keep your kids from getting more serious sniffles and fevers by making sure that they get a flu shot each fall. In fact, kids as young as 6 months can receive a flu shot. "Over 200,000 people go to the hospital and 36,000 people die every year from complications of influenza," says actress Jennifer Garner, mom of two and spokesperson for the American Lung Association's Faces of Influenza Campaign. "And children are more susceptible to getting the flu and developing complications, such as secondary infections, from it." To find a flu clinic in your area, go to facesofinfluenza.org and click on "Flu Clinic Locator."

12 to 14 hours; preschoolers, 11 to 12 hours; and older kids, 10 to 11 hours), help him wind down with a nightly routine, such as putting away toys, taking a bath, and reading a book. "Reading before bed is linked to more sleep," says Mindell. What also helps: cutting the caffeine in his diet by limiting sodas, iced teas, and chocolate.

Dental Checkups: The Right Time to Start

Even if your baby's grin is still mostly toothless, it's a good time to see the dentist. The University of North Carolina found that children who start dental checkups by age 1 need fewer fillings than those who start at age 2 or 3—the ages recommended by the American Academy of Pediatrics. "The dentist can catch potential problems earlier and coach parents on preventive care," says Jessica Y. Lee, D.D.S., author of the study. A bonus: By age 5, dental bills for kids who get their first checkup at age 1 averaged $262, versus $449 for those who first visited a dentist at age 2 or 3.

Safeguard Their Smiles

Pop quiz: What's the number one chronic disease affecting 5- to 17-year-old kids in America today? Give yourself an A+ if you answered tooth decay. More than one-fourth of children ages 2 to 4 have dental decay, and by ages 6 to 8 *half* have cavities, according to the Centers for Disease Control (CDC). The good news? You can help your young ones outsmart dental decay. Here, easy-to-enforce guidelines for keeping kids' smiles bright and beautiful.

What to Do Between Ages 2 and 5

SWITCH TO A "BIG KID" FLUORIDE TOOTHPASTE. Once your child is able to spit, begin using a fluoride toothpaste—but use only a pea-size amount to minimize accidental ingestion. "If your child has trouble hitting the sink, get her a fun, colorful bathroom cup specifically for spitting into," says Robin Lucas, D.M.D., a general and cosmetic dentist in Hoboken, NJ, and a mom of two. "It teaches her to spit in a controlled manner, while catching any wayward foam."

Tooth Fairy Confidential

$2.09: That's the average amount of money the Tooth Fairy gave in 2008 for each tooth a child leaves under his pillow—up 51 cents from 2003—according to Securian Dental, an insurance provider.

MAKE BRUSHING AN ADVENTURE. Many dentists advise two minutes of brushing—one minute on the upper teeth and one on the lower. But try making that happen with a go-go-go toddler. To get yours to keep at it, H. Pitts Hinson, D.D.S., former president of the American Academy of Pediatric Dentistry, suggests playing the "road-map game": Tell him to imagine his toothbrush is an explorer taking a trip around his mouth, and the adventure isn't over until the brush has visited all the teeth, front and back.

What to Do Through Adolescence

SEAL IN HEALTHY TEETH. As your child's permanent molars start erupting, her dentist will determine if she need dental sealants. These adhesive coatings—applied to the molars' crevices and pits—serve as a barrier against tooth-attacking food and bacteria. Unlike fluoride varnish, sealants are being covered by more dental insurance plans. Considering that, according to the CDC, kids who receive sealants have 60 percent fewer new instances of decay in the back teeth (where 90 percent of the decay occurs) for up to five years after a single application, that's news to smile about.

Are Your Kids Getting Too Much Fluoride?

Dental fluorosis—a condition caused by excess fluoride exposure that creates white streaks on teeth—has increased by 9 percent among kids ages 6 to 19 in the past 20 years, according to recent analysis by the CDC. The rise is small—but is it cause for alarm? "There's no evidence of any negative heath effects liked with dental fluorosis," says Mary J. Hayes, D.D.S., an American Dental Association spokesperson. "And fluoride is an invaluable tool against tooth decay."

Sleep

Before having children, did you think much about sleep? Now, after children, do you think much about *anything* else? Here's what you need to know to send your child into dreamland—so you can go there, too.

How Much Sleep Is Enough?

Nearly 70 percent of kids under age 10 experience some type of sleep problem, according to the National Sleep Foundation. And although sleep needs naturally decrease by about 15 minutes on average every year (1-year-olds require almost 14 hours daily, while a 17-year-old needs at least 8.25 hours), a startling 80 percent of kids ages 11 to 17 get less than the recommended amount.

Unfortunately, lost sleep can do more than just leave kids groggy and grumpy. Studies show that children who are sleep-deprived

Why Benadryl Isn't for Bedtime

It's tempting to turn to a sleep aid occasionally when your child's having trouble catching some zzz's, and lots of parents use Benadryl. But researchers at the Johns Hopkins School of Medicine have found that Benadryl actually makes it *harder* for kids to doze off. "Tons of parents give kids Benadryl because it's recommended by many pediatricians and it puts adults to sleep," says Daniel Merenstein, M.D., lead author of the study. "But it doesn't work the same way in young children." The likely reason, says Merenstein, is that one of the drug's side effects—causing hyperactivity—is more pronounced in kids than in adults, canceling any sleep-inducing effect that the medication has. The best sleep aids, he says, are drug-free: Limit caffeinated food and beverages, don't send kids to bed hungry, stick to regular bedtimes, and follow a nighttime routine (such as taking a bath and reading a book), which helps kids wind down and get ready for sleep.

are more likely to be depressed, to catch colds and flu, and to suffer accidents on the playground. Just one hour less of sleep a night causes measurable memory and concentration problems. Behavioral problems, such as whining and short tempers, also shoot up. And those who get less than 10 hours a night are three times more likely to be obese than those getting 12 or more, putting them at higher risk of diabetes and other weight-related conditions.

Help Kids Sleep All Night

Here are five top children's sleep-stealers, plus smart strategies that ensure sound slumber for them—*and* for you.

- **OVERSCHEDULING.** Participation in too many after-school activities can get kids amped up, pushing back dinnertime, homework time—and bedtime. Compared to 1981, now the average kid has almost two hours less of unstructured time each day. Instead, they spend twice as much time in structured competitive sports, while good old-fashioned outdoor play— the running, jumping, and catch-playing that reduces stress and helps them sleep at night—has dropped by more than half. Sleep expert Jodi A. Mindell, Ph.D., suggests, "Sit down with your child and tell him, 'You're allowed to do two things this season: one sport and another activity. Which will it be?'"

- **TOO MUCH TECHNOLOGY.** Kids log six-and-a-half hours a day in front of the television or computer, playing video games, or listening to music—nearly as many hours as they are in school. And the more screens and gadgets kids have in their bedrooms, the more likely they are to doze off at school or over homework. What's more, a recent study showed that TV-watching at bedtime makes kids less likely to drift off into sound, rejuvenating sleep, plus many kids get up and watch TV in the middle of the night, which is likely to amp them up, says Mindell.

Real Advice from Real Moms

Put Nightmares to Bed

"When your child has nightmares, here's how to ward off 'monsters': Use a battery-operated handheld fan to chase them away, and fill a spray bottle with 'Go-Away Monster Spray.' Then lie in bed with your child and ask him what he'd like to dream about, suggesting pleasant things like sharing an ice cream cone or building a sand castle on the beach. This worked with my son, and now he sleeps through the night."

- Have your child go
  to bed and wake up
  at the same time
  each day.
- Use bright lights on
  dark winter mornings
  to help rouse kids.
- Start bedtime prep
  a half hour before
  lights-out.
- Encourage half-hour
  after-school naps to
  help them rejuvenate.

The solution? Make your child's bedroom a media-free zone. If she already has a computer or TV there, unplug it and move it into a family space. Another tactic, one that also boosts health: Have your child "earn" each hour of recreational tech time with an hour of exercise. When researchers at the University of Ottawa employed this strategy with overweight children, it cut the kids' TV time by two hours a day, increased their physical activity by 65 percent, and reduced their body mass index, lowering their risk of weight-related health concerns.

● **SNEAKY CAFFEINE.** Even just one caffeinated drink a day robs children of half an hour of sleep each night—another reason to monitor your child's intake of sugar-laden sodas. But caffeine can lurk in lots of surprising places, including bottled teas, chocolate, and coffee-flavored ice cream. Hefty amounts can also be found in over-the-counter medications such as Anacin, Excedrin, and Dristan, so scan the active and inactive ingredients list for caffeine before you give your child one of these meds. And check drink and protein bar labels for guarana, a common herbal stimulant.

● **NIGHTMARES.** Bad dreams are often triggered by real-life events that frighten kids, including immunizations, being left alone, accidents, or the nightly news report. "Nightmares are actually good for a child. They're a way to process and made sense of both real and imaginary fears, which enables him to deal with them better in his waking life," says pediatrician Alan Greene, M.D., author of *Raising Baby Green* and Clinical Professor of Pediatrics at Stanford University. "If a nightmare wakes him up, your best approach is to comfort him and tuck him back into bed, then give him the opportunity the next day to draw pictures or tell stories to work through the underlying issues."

● **MORE THAN JUST A NIGHTMARE.** If your child screams, moans, or thrashes wildly in the middle of the night, and is glassy-eyed and unresponsive when you try to console him, he is probably

HEALTH

having night terrors—a sign that he's stuck between two stages of non-REM sleep. He won't even remember the event the next morning, so it's better left unmentioned. Night terrors often occur when a child is potty training or overtired, so try leading him to the bathroom or letting him sleep a little longer in the mornings or during naps.

- **A HIDDEN HEALTH CONCERN.** If your child snores heavily off and on, thrashes about in bed, and awakens frequently, her struggles with sleeping may signal an underlying health condition that requires attention. One common culprit: sleep apnea, a condition characterized by temporary breathing disruptions during slumber. (Take a look at page 83 for more information.) Other sneaky sleep-stealers include respiratory problems such as asthma and allergies, as well as restless legs syndrome (a neurological disorder characterized by an uncontrollable urge to move your legs when they're at rest) and narcolepsy (a sleep disorder marked by brief "sleep attacks" that come on during the day).

- If lifestyle changes such as nixing caffeine or moving the TV don't solve your little one's sleeplessness within two to four weeks, see your pediatrician or visit one of 2,000 sleep clinics nationwide to get the proper diagnosis and treatment. For a sleep clinic in your area, log on to sleep-center.org.

Get Your Bed Back!

Many parents bring their child into their bed when they're nursing, or "just for tonight" if a kid's sick or has a nightmare, but one night leads to another and can quickly snowball into a permanent situation, says Lawrence E. Shapiro, Ph.D., author of *A Parent's Guide to Getting Kids Out of the Family Bed*. "Parents often think it's easier to let the co-sleeping continue than to fight with the child about moving back into their own bed," he says. But in addition to giving you alone time with your partner, sending the kids packing also means a good night's sleep for you. Here, Shapiro's tips for giving kids the boot:

- **AVOID SCARY BEDTIME STORIES.** Shapiro suggests that you make up stories about kids finding ways to problem-solve and be independent, rather than fairy tales with pirates and monsters, which might send them running right back to your bed.

- **USE REWARDS.** Tell your child you are starting a fun program to get him used to sleeping in his own bed—and for every night he does so, he will get a sticker or another treat.

- **TEACH SELF-CALMING.** If your child says she can't fall asleep on her own, practice relaxation exercises in the early evening. "Even 2-year-olds can do deep breathing or imagine themselves in their favorite peaceful place," says Shapiro.

- **GET TOUGH.** Sign a contract with your partner in which you state, "We agree that in 21 days, our child will not sleep in our bed," says Shapiro, who suggests you lock your bedroom door or put a child gate in front of your kid's door at night. "There may be a few nights of crying, but after that, everyone will be happier."

What to Do About Bed-wetting

Contrary to popular belief, regular bed-wetting in young kids is not caused by a physical or emotional problem, according to a report from the Canadian Paediatric Society. The real culprit: "Little kids sleep so soundly that they sometimes don't wake up when their bladders are full," says Mark Feldman, M.D., lead author of the report. "As children grow older, their sleep naturally gets lighter, and they stop wetting the bed." Feldman advises against using "treatments" such as alarms that go off when the bed gets wet, medication, or a reward system for dry nights—all of which place undue stress on kids and don't necessarily work. The best approach is to wait it out. While you do, put a plastic mattress pad on your child's bed and avoid giving her caffeine or fluids before she hits the sack. "Most importantly, let your child know that a wet bed isn't her fault," says Feldman. "Explain that she'll outgrow it in time."

Exercise

You know your kids need to exercise, but how can you get them off the couch and out the door? Make exercise fun! It really *is* possible—here's how.

7 Ways to Make Staying Fit Fun

There's no denying it: Thanks to the Internet, video games, cutbacks in physical education, and lackluster after-school childcare programs, children are more sedentary than ever—and their health is paying a huge price. Even the pros—celebrity trainers, nutritionists, psychologists—struggle to keep their own kids moving. But these folks are armed with an arsenal of tools and tactics learned on the job for encouraging healthy habits. Here, seven experts (who are also parents) share their insider knowledge for raising a fit child.

Make playtime a family affair.

"Instead of watching TV on rainy days, I set time limits on sedentary activities and alternate them with 'Bins of Fun.' We have several bins with active toys, including jump ropes, Hula-Hoops, Hacky Sacks, etc., and we all play. And when the yard needs tidying, we play 'Trash Dash.' I assign a job to each family member, set the timer, and we try to clean up the yard in under X minutes flat."

DEBI PILLARELLA, M.ED.
CERTIFIED PERSONAL TRAINER AND AMERICAN COUNCIL
ON EXERCISE YOUTH FITNESS SPOKESPERSON

Mix it up with mini workouts.

"I created a one-minute workout for my kids called JAM (Just a Minute). It involves doing a series of five simple exercises such as toe touches and hopping on one foot for one minute. You can change up the exercises, and, ideally, get them to do it more than once a day. I've got teachers doing JAM sessions in the classroom: They say that it improves kids' attention spans and they aren't as wiggly."

KATHY KAEHLER
CELEBRITY FITNESS TRAINER AND AUTHOR OF
FIT AND AND SEXY FOR LIFE

Invest in a healthy lifestyle.

"We hired a company called Sport Court to set up a tiled surface outside our home where the kids can play tennis, roller hockey, and volleyball. Sports courts can be pricey, but think about how much so many of us are willing to put out for entertainment and the latest Xbox. Dollar for dollar, you can't match the return you get when you bring the family together and increase activity level."

GUNNAR PETERSON
CERTIFIED STRENGTH AND CONDITIONING SPECIALIST
AND AUTHOR OF *THE WORKOUT*

Make this video game the good guy.

"Our kids were begging for Dance Dance Revolution Max, but we kept putting it off—until I saw it in action. It's a dancing video game that comes with a floor pad. You choose a level of difficulty, and the game plays music and provides visual cues that show you how to do dance moves. My kids love to bring it out when friends are over."

BRIDGET SWINNEY, R.D.
AUTHOR OF *HEALTHY FOOD FOR HEALTHY KIDS*

Get them in the swim.

"We try to include things on our vacations. For instance, we always stay at hotels with pools. After driving in the car for several hours, the kids race for the pool as soon as we check in. It's teaching them to know what to do with their pent-up energy."

ANN KEARNEY-COOKE, PH.D.
AUTHOR OF *CHANGE YOUR MIND, CHANGE YOUR BODY*

Lead by example.

"They say that kids retain 15 percent of what they hear, and 85 percent of what they see. So it's essential that parents be good fitness role models. I work out with my kids regularly, plus I try to provide an environment with lots of opportunity to exercise. In fact, that's the reason we moved recently: Now we're two minutes from hiking trails and we're also near the ocean. Our new house is smaller, but a fit lifestyle is more accessible to the whole family."

ROB PARR
PERSONAL AND CELEBRITY TRAINER
AND FITNESS CONSULTANT

Make exercise easy for everyone.

"Instead of letting lethargy set in after dinner, we try to get an extra spurt of energy by throwing a football around or shooting some baskets. We also love Aerobie Discs. You can really make them zip without much skill, so they're great for the nonathletically inclined."

BONNIE FASS-OFFIT, M.D.
PEDIATRICIAN AT KIDS FIRST-HAVERFORD
THE CHILDREN'S HOSPITAL OF PHILADELPHIA

Symptoms

Your child has a fever and a runny nose. Is it a cold? The flu? Allergies? What about that headache he's had on and off for a few days? Should you take him to the doctor or let it ride its course? How can a mom without a medical degree know what to do? Simply consult the information below!

5 Symptoms Moms Can Relax About
(And 4 to Never Ignore)

Ever wish you had a live-in pediatrician to tell you exactly what to do when your child is sick? Here's the next best thing for your peace of mind: a doctor-approved guide to when symptoms are harmless—and when they're not.

Wait-and-see symptoms

FEVER. A temperature is really just a sign that your child's body is fighting an infection, which does not necessarily require a run to the doctor. "Some parents have heard that their child will have brain damage with a 103- or 104-degree fever, but a high fever won't cause harm to the child," says Tanya Remer Altmann, M.D., a pediatrician in West Lake Village, CA. In fact, it's not unusual for young kids to have a temperature of up to 104 for four or five days. You can ease your child's discomfort and bring down his temperature by giving him acetaminophen or ibuprofen (for kids older than 6 months). Contrary to popular belief, lowering a fever will not prolong the illness.

The exception is a fever in newborns under 2 months of age, which could signal a serious infection. "If that happens, parents should call their pediatrician no matter what time of day or night," says Ellen Putter, M.D., a pediatrician in New York City. Older kids should see a doctor if their fever is accompanied by listlessness or inconsolable irritability, or if their temperature spikes to 105 degrees.

COUGH. Like the common cold, most coughs are caused by a viral infection, which must run its course—and which no medication will cure. The best remedy for this kind of cough is to make sure your child drinks lots of fluids and gets plenty of rest, then wait for the cough to resolve itself.

A cough that lasts for more than two weeks, continuously disrupts your child's sleep, or causes her to take short, rapid breaths or have trouble catching her breath could signal an allergy, pneumonia, bronchitis, or asthma—and should be checked out by a doctor, says Ari Brown, M.D., a pediatrician in Austin, TX, and coauthor of *Baby 411*. If the cough sounds like high-pitched barking and your child's breathing is labored, it may be croup, which occurs when the windpipe is inflamed. Ten minutes in a steamy bathroom should relieve the swelling, but if your child continues to have difficulty breathing, you'll need to go to the ER so she can be treated with steroids to relax the airway.

RASH. When red blotches appear on your child's skin, it's usually due to one of four causes, none of which are serious: a viral infection (which will most often resolve itself); a reaction to a skin irritant such as soap or poison ivy (known as contact dermatitis); a reaction to an allergen such as perfume; or dry skin (all of which can be diagnosed as eczema). Contact dermatitis looks like a patch or streak of blisters where the skin rubbed against the allergen, while eczema looks like dry, red, rough patches of skin, usually appearing on the elbows and knees. Moisturizing the area and skipping soap during baths will help alleviate the itchiness from contact dermatitis and eczema, but you'll also need to uncover the irritant or allergen. "The distribution of the rash can be a clue," says Brown. "Dots that match up to where the snaps on a pair of pajamas fall might indicate sensitivity to the metal." Rashes that occur when your child plays with a person who's wearing perfume could be due to the fragrance. If you can't zero in on the allergen and the rash has gone on for more than a week, consult your pediatrician. Turn to page 87 for more information.

More than 10 million American kids suffer from chronic headaches, but thankfully, the cure to their pain may be right there in their own heads. As wacky as it may sound, when children were taught self-hypnosis, they were actually able to significantly decrease the frequency, duration, and intensity of their headaches, found researchers at the University of Minnesota—good news for parents who are looking for alternatives to medication.

Children may be particularly open to this method, says the study's lead author, Daniel P. Kohen, M.D., "because they understand that hypnosis is a state similar to imagination or daydreaming." In the study, children suffering from headaches were taught to get into a hypnotic state and then use personalized imagery, such as picturing a place where they had never had headaches or imagining their pain slowly decreasing as a number on a ruler. They were then advised to practice the technique at home for 10 or 15 minutes twice a day. Want to find a doctor or therapist near you who's trained in hypnosis? Log on to asch.net.

HEADACHES. "When kids complain of headaches, parents often think, Oh, my God, my child has meningitis," says Putter. "But headaches are very common—they even happen in toddlers." You can give your child acetaminophen or ibuprofen to relieve the pain, but the best way to get rid of headaches in the long run is to figure out what the trigger is, and eliminate it. The usual culprits, says Putter, are lack of sleep, vision problems, allergies, or simply hunger. If your child gets headaches first thing in the morning for several days in a row and has blurred vision or vomiting, however, consult your pediatrician. This combination of symptoms could indicate a tumor in the brain.

UNUSUAL BOWEL MOVEMENTS. The frequency and makeup of poop vary greatly depending on a child's age and diet. Breast-fed newborns generally poop more often than formula-fed babies; older kids can poop from twice a day to once every three days. And it's all fine. "Nonetheless, parents frequently fret that their kids aren't pooping enough, are pooping too often, or that the color is strange," says Altmann. But even poop that's out of the

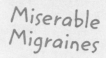

Migraines aren't just for grown-ups. Up to 10 percent of kids get them, usually between the ages of 8 and 14, according to a recent article in the journal *Pediatrics*.

"A lot of children with migraines are misdiagnosed with tension headaches, which delays getting them the right treatment," says Jacques Bruijn, M.D., a coauthor of the article and a pediatric neurologist in the Netherlands. If your child has a migraine, he'll have a pulsating headache, and won't be able to do any activity. Acetaminophen or ibuprofen should ease his pain, but the prescription nasal spray sumatriptan works faster. To help prevent migraines, jot down what was going on when the headaches occurred, and cut the culprits. Some common triggers: lack of sleep, chocolate and sweets, stressful life events, or tests at school.

ordinary rarely indicates an illness, unless there's blood in it—which could mean an intestinal infection. If your child goes four days without pooping, he's probably constipated, in which case a diet of more fruits, veggies, water, prune juice, and whole grains should fix him right up.

Call-the-doctor symptoms

WEIGHT LOSS. Unless your child is overweight and trying to slim down to get healthier, infants and children should never lose weight. "A growing kid should be gaining weight every month," says Vincent Iannelli, M.D., a pediatrician in Dallas. "It's okay for your child to lose a pound or two for a day or two when he's sick, but it's not normal if your child continues to lose weight over several weeks." Significant weight loss—which Iannelli defines as 5 percent of body weight—could be an indication of diabetes or cancer. As a general rule, kids should gain about two pounds a month for the first three months, a pound a month until they're 12 months old, ½ a pound to ¾ a pound a month to age 2, and then four pounds a year until puberty.

THIRST AND FREQUENT URINATION. It makes sense that if a child drinks a lot, he'll pee a lot. But if your child is also losing weight quickly or shedding pounds despite regular eating habits, she could have diabetes, an increasingly common endocrine disorder in kids. Frequent urination could also be a sign of a urinary tract infection, which must be treated with antibiotics.

SLEEP DISTURBANCES. Yes, kids will have good nights and bad nights sleeping. A child who never seems to get restful sleep, and breathes through her mouth most of the night, however, may have sleep apnea. The condition, which occurs when enlarged tonsil tissue or adenoids (germ-fighting tissues in the back of the throat) obstruct your child's airway, is occasionally dangerous, so have it checked out. Either way, it can make your child miserable since she could be prone to frequent sinus infections and runny nose, not to mention crankiness and low energy due to lack of sleep, says Brown. Depending on how severe your child's case is, she may need the enlarged tissue to be surgically removed so she can sleep and function better.

BIG BELLY. It's easy to dismiss a protruding tummy as the result of a big meal or gas. But a large stomach could indicate an intolerance of gluten, which will require that your child abstain from gluten-rich foods such as wheat, rye, and barley. A distended belly could even be a sign of leukemia, or cancers of the abdominal cavity. If your child has a serious illness, the shape of his tummy will resemble that of a pregnant woman's—jutting out lower down—and his belly will remain big for three or four days. Another tip-off: If you press on your child's protruding belly while he's lying down and it feels firm, it might be a problem," says Brown. Of course, "might" is the operative word here. Follow your instincts: Anytime you're unsure and anxious about your child's symptoms—whether it's a big belly or a nagging cough—call your pediatrician.

Which Illness Is It?

Lots of common ailments have befuddlingly similar symptoms. Here's how to tell the difference and how to help your child start feeling better.

Cold, flu, or allergies?

? **IT MAY BE A COLD IF . . .** your child is up and about, even if she has a runny nose, congestion, sneezing, a sore throat, and a cough. Symptoms tend to come on slowly and last no more than two weeks, says Sara Caldararo, M.D., an assistant professor of clinical pediatrics at The Albert Einstein College of Medicine in Bronx, NY. If your child does have a fever, it's typically low-grade. Some kids may have mild aches, including headaches.

✔ **WHAT TO DO:** Make sure your child gets plenty of fluids and rest. Try a cool-mist humidifier to relieve congestion. Cold symptoms that last several weeks—especially if your child has a headache, a low-grade fever, and (for an older child) facial pain—may signal a sinus infection, which requires antibiotics.

? **IT MAY BE THE FLU IF . . .** your child is listless—and grumpy. "They're miserable because they just feel so bad," says Carol Steltenkamp, M.D., an associate professor of pediatrics at the University of Kentucky. The flu comes on quickly, and symptoms include chills, fatigue, muscle aches, and a fever.

✔ **WHAT TO DO:** To reduce fever and relieve aches or pain, try giving your child acetaminophen or ibuprofen (both of which are considered safe for children over the age of 6 months). If you take your child to the pediatrician within 48 hours after

Snoring and Allergies

Your kid's snoring may seem harmless, maybe even a little cute. But her nighttime saw sounds could be a reaction to allergens like ragweed, mold, and dust. An Australian study suggests that snoring is linked to childhood allergies, and among children with rhinitis (a stuffy, runny, or itchy nose), 60 percent snored at least once a week. "Snoring causes disrupted sleep, which can lead to problems with learning and behavior," says Bradley Chipps, M.D., a pediatric allergist in Sacramento, CA. Talk to your pediatrician if your child snores. Keep your child's room dust-free by using protective coverings, vacuuming, and removing cloth curtains, stuffed toys, and flannel sheets. And avoid using a humidifier; it'll only promote more dust and mold.

symptoms start, he may prescribe an antiviral remedy that can decrease the flu's duration. If symptoms don't improve after 10 days, the fever continues to climb, or your child starts having trouble breathing or drinking enough fluids, call your doctor—she may have something more serious, such as pneumonia.

IT MAY BE ALLERGIES IF . . . your child feels itchy in her eyes, nose, or both, and has nasal congestion and sneezing, but never a fever. Colds go away in 7 to 14 days, but allergies can hang on indefinitely, especially if your child is sensitive to indoor allergens, like dust mites and mold.

WHAT TO DO: Oral antihistamines, like Benadryl and Claritin, can usually provide some symptom relief. Head to your doctor to get a sense of how intense your kid's allergies are and ask about intra-nasal steroid sprays, such as Flonase, which can prevent allergy symptoms, says Derek Johnson, M.D., a pediatric allergy and immunology specialist in Fairfax, VA. "Use mattress and pillow encasements to shield your child from dust allergens and wash bedding and stuffed toys in hot water to kill dust mites," he says. "Keep pets out of the bedroom and don't use humidifiers, which will only encourage mold and dust mite growth."

Viral sore throat or strep throat?

IT MAY BE A VIRAL SORE THROAT IF . . . your child also has coldlike symptoms such as nasal congestion, cough, and hoarseness. The same viruses that cause colds cause sore throats, too.

WHAT TO DO: Treat the pain with sore-throat lozenges, a warm salt-water gargle, or acetaminophen or ibuprofen—and make sure your child gets plenty of fluids and rest.

IT MAY BE STREP THROAT IF . . . the throat pain is accompanied by headache, stomachache, and swollen glands in the neck. Strep throat is a bacterial infection which, unlike a viral infection, doesn't cause coldlike symptoms. But in some cases, strep brings on a rash that may spread to the entire body; this is known as scarlet fever.

✔ **WHAT TO DO**: Take your child to the pediatrician. Any time your child has a sore throat *without* respiratory symptoms, consult your doctor, Caldararo says. He may test for strep and prescribe an antibiotic.

Whooping cough or croup?

❓ **IT MAY BE WHOOPING COUGH IF** . . . your child's cough is persistent and sounds as if he's choking. Also known as pertussis, whooping cough occurs when bacteria attack the airways and they swell and narrow as a result. Whooping cough is rare; kids are usually immunized against it with a series of shots between 6 months and 6 years. But the disease still occurs in infants who haven't received all their immunizations yet—and in puberty, when the vaccine starts to wear off. "Pertussis acts like a cold for a week or two, and then the cough gets worse, and the child may begin to breathe more rapidly," says Debbie Thompson, a pediatric nurse practitioner. "The cough persists until the child is completely out of breath—they can even begin to turn blue as a result of not getting enough oxygen."

✔ **WHAT TO DO**: See your pediatrician immediately for antibiotics. Infants with severe breathing problems may need to be hospitalized.

❓ **IT MAY BE CROUP IF** . . . the cough sounds like a bark. Croup is a viral infection of the upper airway that tends to occur in kids under 5 during the winter. It may start as a cold, with a cough that worsens at night.

✔ **WHAT TO DO**: With the shower running, have your child inhale hot, steamy air, then take him outdoors into the cold. "If it stops the cough it may be croup," Steltenkamp says. Some experts believe that the quick dilation and constriction of the airways helps relieve the cough. If it doesn't, your child may have pneumonia with a cough. Croup usually lasts only a few days and doesn't require treatment. But if you see him struggling to breathe, take him to the ER immediately.

Impetigo or contact dermatitis?

? IT MAY BE IMPETIGO IF . . . there are pustules or blisters that break and scab over with a crust. Impetigo is a bacterial skin infection usually caused by staph that enters through an abrasion, cut, or insect bite. It tends to occur on the face or extremities and isn't itchy.

✓ WHAT TO DO: See your pediatrician for a prescription antibiotic cream such as mupirocin. If the impetigo is widespread, your child may require oral antibiotics. "Infants—who have weaker immune systems—should be brought to a doctor, even if there's only a few pustules," Caldararo says. Impetigo is contagious, so avoid sharing towels, linens, and clothing. Also, keep your child away from other kids, and wash hands frequently.

? IT MAY BE CONTACT DERMATITIS IF . . . your child is scratching at dry and thickened skin. The dermatitis typically shows up where the skin has made contact with an allergen, such as poison ivy, nickel (found in jewelry or clothing snaps), or the fragrances and preservatives in topical lotions.

✓ WHAT TO DO: Wash the area well. Relieve the itch with an over-the-counter cortisone cream or an oral antihistamine, like Benadryl. If the rash is widespread, is on the genitalia, or causes facial swelling, call your pediatrician, says Daniel Krowchuk, M.D., a professor of pediatrics at Wake Forest University. Your child may need an oral steroid, such as prednisone, to get rid of the rash.

Medication

Your child is sick and you want him to get better—but are antibiotics the answer? Not always, as you'll discover here, along with some common myths about medicine you need to avoid.

To Medicate or Not? That is the Question

How do you know when antibiotics are needed and when they're overkill? Here, six common childhood ailments—and the safest, most effective ways to treat them.

Colds/flu. Both of these dreaded bugs are caused by viruses, not bacteria, so antibiotics won't help—not even when the gunk from his nose turns yellow or green (a symptom many people believe is a sign of bacterial infection). And while it's true that a cold can lead to sinus infection (more on that below), antibiotics won't help head one off. The best treatment approach: rest, fluids (to keep sinuses draining), an over-the-counter fever-reducer (such as ibuprofen), a decongestant before bed, and a cool-mist humidifier (to soothe inflamed sinuses).

Sinus infections (sinusitis). A cold can last up to two weeks, but if your child's symptoms don't improve after 10 days and she's suffering from coughing, puffy eyes, fever, headache, and/or facial pain, there's a good chance she's developed a bacterial sinus infection. It's impossible to diagnose a sinus infection from a physical exam alone (other triggers, like allergies, can cause similar symptoms), so your pediatrician will also consider symptom duration.

Stop Infection in its Tracks

The best way to avoid giving your kids too many antibiotics? Help them stay well to begin with. Some quick tips:

- Teach kids to wash their hands with soap and warm water after playing and before eating. They should scrub for 30 seconds (long enough for one round of "Twinkle, Twinkle, Little Star").
- Use alcohol-based hand wipes or hand gels when you can't get to a sink. Avoid those with triclosan, an antibacterial agent that kills only weaker bacteria.

- Show your child how to cough into her sleeve, and use tissues instead of her hands to wipe her nose.
- Have each family member use his or her own towel.
- Clean all wounds properly: Flush for one minute with running water, wash with soap, rinse, and cover with a bandage until healed.
- Make sure your child receives all four Prevnar vaccinations (to fight off seven strains of bacterial pneumonia). There have been periods of shortages since the vaccine's release, so some kids didn't get all four doses.

If all signs point toward a sinus infection, it's time for amoxicillin, the most effective antibiotic for this type of infection.

Ear infections. When doctors diagnose an ear infection, they're often referring to otitis media with effusion (OME), which strikes 90 percent of children at least once before school age. Characterized by fluid buildup in the middle ear and inflammation in the inner ear, OME typically doesn't involve bacteria and resolves on its own within three months. Another type of ear infection, known as acute otitis media (AOM), *can* involve bacteria—but up to 80 percent of cases clear up without treatment within a few days.

Even so, when your little one complains of ear pain, see a pediatrician. "It may be a symptom of other conditions, such as strep throat or infections of the neck or brain," says Kenneth A. Alexander, M.D., a pediatric infectious-disease specialist at the University of Chicago. If your pediatrician suspects AOM, but your child is 3 or older and hasn't had an ear infection in the last year, the best treatment is an OTC pain reliever along with watchful waiting. Any increase in pain or continuing fever after 48 hours requires an ear recheck. Kids under 3, or those with chronic ear infections or other signs of illness, will likely be given amoxicillin.

Strep throat. Antibiotics are a must for strep, a throat infection caused by streptococcus bacteria, since untreated cases can lead to swelling joints or heart damage. But not all sore throats are strep, so it's essential that your pediatrician perform a throat culture to determine the cause. If the test is positive, penicillin is a smart choice: So far, strep shows no signs of being resistant to it. However, it tastes awful, so most doctors will prescribe better-tasting amoxicillin or Omnicef to up the odds that kids will take it.

Bronchitis. A hacking cough brought on by inflammation in the airways leading to the lungs, bronchitis is almost always a result of the cold virus, so it rarely requires antibiotics, according to the Centers for Disease Control and Prevention (CDC). Hard to believe, since the cough can linger for weeks and even months—long after the virus itself is gone—as the lungs heal. But if it's accompanied by other symptoms such as headache and facial pain, the virus may have brought on a sinus infection (see above). A fever may indicate bacterial pneumonia, which does require antibiotics and can be confirmed with a chest X-ray (but these infections are rare).

Staph infections. Telltale signs of a skin staphylococcus (staph) infection include an inflamed area with a pimple in the center, pus oozing from the area, and fever. "It's often mistaken for a spider bite," says Gregory Storch, M.D., head of the division of infectious disease at St. Louis Children's Hospital, so see your pediatrician if your child develops these symptoms. Although some infections occur when staph enters an open cut, often there's no visible break in the skin.

Unfortunately, in many communities in the United States, more than 50 percent of staph bacteria are resistant to many oral antibiotics, so diagnosing a resistant strain early can ensure that your child gets the most effective antibiotic from the get-go. Insist on a culture to determine the bacterial strain and correct corresponding antibiotic treatment.

The Top 5 Medicine Myths

Parents often follow common medicine practices that sometimes don't help kids feel better. In fact, they can wind up making kids feel far worse. "We suspect that parents make mistakes fairly frequently when giving medicine to their kids," says Richard Gorman, M.D., the Clinical Associate Professor of Pediatrics for the University of Maryland School of Medicine. "Doctors call these 'therapeutic misadventures.'" How can you avoid such misadventures? See if you've been guided by any of the following myths, then take our advice on what to do instead.

Myth 1

When your child is in pain, give her both acetaminophen and ibuprofen to provide relief, fast.

THE REAL DEAL: *Double-dosing doesn't deliver quicker relief.* When a child is in a lot of pain, some pediatricians recommend giving her full doses of both drugs at the same time. However, "there's no added fever or pain control," says Gorman. What's more, "you have the chance of getting the side effects from both medicines." These include an irritated stomach or, worse, kidney problems, because both drugs can decrease blood flow to the kidneys. And in rare cases, if your child becomes dehydrated—say, if she has a fever or stomach virus—she could develop kidney failure, which can be fatal.

WHAT TO DO: Stick with whichever drug eases your child's pain best. A study at Sydney Children's Hospital in Australia found that ibuprofen and acetaminophen were similarly effective at treating moderate to severe pain in kids. If neither drug soothes your child, ask if something stronger (acetaminophen with codeine, for instance, is sometimes given for pain after surgery) or a combination of different types of drugs (say, pain reliever plus a topical anesthetic for an ear infection) is needed.

Myth 2

Use your child's age to determine the correct pain-medication dosage.

THE REAL DEAL: *His weight is a better gauge.* While most over-the-counter drugs offer dosage guidelines by age, pain relievers list them by age *and* weight so you can fine-tune the dose for your child (giving him too much could lead to serious complications). But which do most parents go by? You guessed it—age. The problem is, if your child is big or heavy for his age, you might underdose him, which means he might continue to feel miserable, and you might think his illness is worse than it really is. On the other hand, if your child is small or thin for his age, you could overdose him. Repeated, around-the-clock overdosing with ibuprofen can cause abdominal pain and, in rare cases, gastrointestinal bleeding, and too much acetaminophen can cause liver damage or liver failure. (And, as mentioned before, too much of either one can cause kidney problems.)

✔ **WHAT TO DO:** When a drug offers dosages by weight, follow it.

Myth 3

If your child has green nasal discharge, she needs an antibiotic.

→ **THE REAL DEAL:** *It could be a sign of a run-of-the-mill cold, which won't respond to antibiotics.* If the color of your child's mucus changes from clear and watery to thicker and white and then to greenish-yellow over several days, your child probably has a common cold, which is caused by a virus and won't respond to antibiotics. Green nasal discharge can also simply be a sign of mucus buildup, especially in small children who cannot blow their noses, says Robert A. Fink, M.D., a pediatrician in Chesapeake, Virginia. Why? The bacteria that normally live in the nose can cause discoloration of the mucus—a harmless (but icky) condition.

✔ **WHAT TO DO:** If your child has persistent or worsening symptoms—say, she has a head cold and then gets a fever or cough—she may have a sinus infection, which requires antibiotics. If a young child seems only to have a cold with greenish mucus, rinse her nose with saltwater nose drops to keep her nasal passages clear.

Myth 4

If your child has a cold, help him shake it faster by giving him cold medicine.

→ **THE REAL DEAL:** *It's not a cure.* "In children, these medicines cause little to no change in symptoms," says Gorman, "and they won't make a cold go away any faster than it would naturally." What cold medicines can do—unfortunately—is cause

---

He Threw Up His Medicine. Now What?

If he vomits within 30 minutes of taking an over-the-counter drug:

- "If he throws up much of what he ate in the past few hours, and you see the drug's color in the vomit, repeat the dosage in half an hour," says Fink.

- If he throws up a small amount, or you don't see the color of the drug in his vomit, ask your doctor what to do.

- If he vomits without previous signs of stomach upset, he could have had a reaction to the drug or the dyes in it. Ask your doctor if he needs to have food with his medication or if he needs a different drug altogether.

- If he vomits more than 30 minutes after taking a drug, assume he absorbed the medicine. Don't repeat the dose.

a number of side effects, especially in young children. Decongestants (particularly those containing pseudoephedrine) can cause nervousness, trembling, or hyperactivity in little ones, and keep older kids up *waaay* past bedtime, says Mary Hegenbarth, M.D., a pediatric emergency physician at Children's Mercy Hospital in Kansas City, MO. Some antihistamines can also cause restlessness in children, rather than the drowsiness you might expect.

✅ **WHAT TO DO:** When your child has a cold, help him breathe easier by keeping his head elevated while he's in bed, and run a cool-mist humidifier in his room at night. Encourage him to blow his nose regularly and to drink lots of clear fluids, such as diluted juices and chicken soup.

Myth 5

If your child has diarrhea, you should give her juice to keep her hydrated or use an antidiarrheal medicine to stop the runs.

➡️ **THE REAL DEAL:** *Both moves can make the diarrhea worse.* Keeping your child hydrated when she has diarrhea is important, but *how* you do it is critical. Certain juices—such as apple and purple grape juice—can make diarrhea worse because they contain high levels of sorbitol, a natural form of sugar that can lead to soft stools. Antidiarrheal drugs aren't such a great idea, either. "Most cases of diarrhea in kids are caused by an intestinal virus, and some medicines prevent the body from flushing out these germs," explains Fink. So the tummy bug could end up staying in your child's system, causing her to be sick a few days longer than if she'd gone medicine-free.

✅ **WHAT TO DO:** Keep your child well hydrated while she battles the infection by giving her plenty of clear liquids, such as water, diluted juice (white grape is a good one), or an electrolyte solution (such as Pedialyte or Gatorade). Another good move: Follow the reliable BRAT diet—bananas, rice, applesauce, and toast—to help firm up her stool.

Warm Weather Worries

Tick bites, sunburns, bee stings: Summer can really do a number on your child. Here's how to treat and prevent the season's inevitable bites, burns, rashes, and more.

How to Treat—and Prevent—Summer's Top Kid Injuries

Knowing what to do about bee stings, heat stress, and other common summer afflictions can save you a trip to the emergency room—and help your child feel better faster.

Bee stings

Warmer weather marks the start of bee season—and bee stings. As many as half of all children will be stung at some point during childhood.

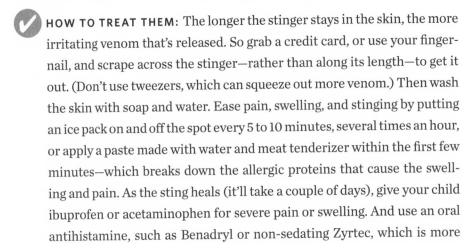 **HOW TO TREAT THEM:** The longer the stinger stays in the skin, the more irritating venom that's released. So grab a credit card, or use your fingernail, and scrape across the stinger—rather than along its length—to get it out. (Don't use tweezers, which can squeeze out more venom.) Then wash the skin with soap and water. Ease pain, swelling, and stinging by putting an ice pack on and off the spot every 5 to 10 minutes, several times an hour, or apply a paste made with water and meat tenderizer within the first few minutes—which breaks down the allergic proteins that cause the swelling and pain. As the sting heals (it'll take a couple of days), give your child ibuprofen or acetaminophen for severe pain or swelling. And use an oral antihistamine, such as Benadryl or non-sedating Zyrtec, which is more

effective than creams, to get rid of hives (if your child develops them) and any itchiness. "Excessive scratching can lead to infection," says Gary Smith, M.D., a pediatric emergency physician in Columbus, OH.

HOW TO PREVENT THEM: Avoid scented soaps, sunscreens, and shampoos—all of which are bee magnets. And be extra careful when eating outdoors. "Bees love to hide inside containers, so never sip from a straw or drink from a can or bottle that's been sitting out," says David B. K. Golden, a Baltimore area allergist.

WHEN TO SEE A DOCTOR: Your child is having a serious allergic reaction if he has difficulty breathing, is breathing rapidly, or becomes suddenly weak or dizzy. Use an EpiPen (an injectable syringe of epinephrine), if available, or call 911.

Tick bites

Camping, hiking, and biking—even hanging out in a tree-filled backyard—can mean an encounter with disease-carrying ticks, who breed and live in wooded areas.

HOW TO TREAT THEM: Unlike a bee's stinger, a tick can be removed with tweezers. Grasp it by the head and pull it straight out, making sure there are no stray tick parts left in the skin. Then wash the area with soap and water, and allow the wound to heal. Never use folklore methods like nail polish remover, matches, or a lighted cigarette to remove a tick. They don't work, and you'll burn or irritate your child's skin. If she was bitten in a region that's known for a tick-transmitted disease—Lyme disease in the Northeast; Rocky Mountain spotted fever in the Midwest and the South Atlantic—save the tick and have your pediatrician test it, to be on the safe side, says Smith.

HOW TO PREVENT THEM: Have your child wear lightweight long-sleeve shirts and pants when she's out in a wooded area. Apply a thin coat of bug repellent to her exposed parts, such as the hands and neck. Repellents with DEET, an insect pesticide, are the most effective, but always use the smallest amount possible (and only on kids older than 2 months). "Ten percent DEET is effective for two hours; 24 percent DEET, for five hours," says Laura A. Jana, M.D., pediatrician and co-founder of the Dr. Spock Company. Jana warns against DEET-and-sunscreen combos, since reapplying to maintain sun protection means way too much DEET exposure.

WHEN TO SEE A DOCTOR: If your child has flulike symptoms, a red rash, or joint pain, have her checked for a tick-borne illness.

Mosquito bites

When it's hot and humid, these bloodsucking insects are out in full force looking for their next meal. A lakeside family picnic at sunset (mosquitoes love nighttime) means these critters get to dine, too!

HOW TO TREAT THEM: Use a cool compress to soothe the itching and swelling. You can make your own anti-itch paste out of equal parts baking soda, water, vinegar, and salt—or try a half-percent hydrocortisone cream or calamine lotion. Since scratching can lead to infection, try an oral antihistamine or keep the bites covered by clothing or a bandage if your child can't keep his hands off.

HOW TO PREVENT THEM: Mosquitoes breed in still water, so always empty the baby pool at the end of each day, and don't let water sit in empty flowerpots or on outdoor toys. Avoid using scented products on your child, and use an insect repellent for added protection.

WHEN TO SEE A DOCTOR: Bites that are warm to the touch and extremely swollen or red after two days could be infected, requiring a prescription topical antibiotic.

Sunburns

The sun is stronger today than it was in your childhood, thanks to a thinning ozone layer that lets more cancer-causing UV rays reach us. "Skin can burn within *minutes* when exposed to summer sunlight between 10 a.m. and 4 p.m.," says Julie Anne Winfield, M.D., a Marin County, CA, pediatric dermatologist. Getting just one sunburn in childhood doubles the risk of getting skin cancer later.

How Do You Get Sunblock on a Squirmy Kid?

"I ask my kids what 'flavor' they want on each arm and leg—picking the flavor gets them totally interested! As I rub the lotion on, I'll pretend: 'Yum, this is vanilla on your left leg, and this is strawberry on your right.'"

"My husband pretends the sunscreen bottle is a bird, and he holds it overhead and makes sound effects. The kids can't wait to find out where it will plop, and they laugh and say 'Eeww' as it gets rubbed in. It may sound gross, but it works!"

✅ **HOW TO TREAT THEM:** A cool compress will soothe red, inflamed skin until the burn heals. Use over-the-counter pain relievers if your child is really uncomfortable.

❌ **HOW TO PREVENT THEM:** Apply a sunblock with an SPF of no lower than 30 on your child about 15 minutes before he heads out. And even if the sunblock is waterproof or water-resistant, reapply it at least every two hours or after excessive sweating or a swim, because some lotion does wash off. When choosing a sunblock, look for the term "broad spectrum," which means it will shut out harmful UVA *and* UVB rays. If your child has sensitive skin, try lotions with zinc oxide or titanium dioxide, which are mild. Sunblocks that are made especially for kids tend to be hypoallergenic.

➕ **WHEN TO SEE A DOCTOR:** If your child's been burned over most of his body, or his burn is blistering or oozing, he probably needs oral steroids or an antibiotic.

Heat stress

The signs of overheating can be hard to recognize, because instead of feeling hot, your child's skin will feel cool and clammy. She may also be weak, dizzy, nauseous, and complain of headache.

✅ **HOW TO TREAT IT:** Find a cool, shaded area (or bring her indoors if there's air-conditioning), and apply cool washcloths to her forehead and the back of her neck to lower her core body temperature. Offer her sips of water, a sports drink, or ice chips so she can begin to rehydrate. Before allowing her to go back out to play, call your pediatrician. "She may need IV replacement fluids, depending on how severe her symptoms were," says Jana.

❌ **HOW TO PREVENT IT:** On hot, humid days, your child needs twice the liquid she normally drinks when spending time outdoors, says Gary Gardner, M.D., a Darien, IL-based pediatrician.

A rough guide: Kids weighing 40 pounds or less should drink a couple of ounces of water every 20 minutes, those weighing 40 to 88 pounds need 5 ounces, and kids weighing more than 132 pounds need 9 ounces.

➕ **WHEN TO SEE A DOCTOR:** Get emergency help if your child is breathing rapidly, has a temperature of more than 105 degrees, or if her skin feels dry—all of which indicate heatstroke, which is life-threatening.

Swimmer's ear

The more time a kid spends in the water, the greater the chance that water will build up in the outer ear canal, where bacteria can grow and cause an infection. The classic signs of the illness: red, swollen earlobes that are sensitive to the touch, and pain inside the ear.

✔ **HOW TO TREAT IT:** An over-the-counter antibiotic ear drop should get rid of the infection. Meanwhile, to soothe the pain, place a hot-water bottle on the ear, or give your child acetaminophen or ibuprofen.

✖ **HOW TO PREVENT IT:** Keep swim time to under an hour if your child's prone to the infection and gets swimmer's ear a few times a season. Have him wear earplugs, and dry out his ears after each swim by wiping his outer ear with a cotton ball dipped in a vinegar-and-water mixture. Don't use cotton swabs; their skinny shape and hard texture make it all too easy to accidentally enter the inner ear canal and puncture the eardrum.

➕ **WHEN TO SEE A DOCTOR:** If your child complains of painful earaches but shows no physical signs of swimmer's ear, have him examined to see if he actually has an inner ear infection, which may require antibiotics.

Real Advice from Real Moms

How Do You Get Sunblock on a Squirmy Kid?

"I use a SunBlankie— it's basically a wipe with sunblock 'soaked in,' so it goes on very quickly. It's pricey, but I've found that one SunBlankie usually covers two kids, and they fit really neatly into diaper bags."

"I make up a story about how Dora or Clifford is going out to play and needs to put on sunscreen for protection. I get really into it, using different voices. If all else fails, a game of tickle monster or a chocolate bribe almost always works."

What's Up with That Rash?

As temperatures rise, so do nasty rashes. Here's what causes some of kids' most common summer skin problems and how to treat (and even prevent) them.

Eczema

Eczema is a chronic skin problem marked by redness, flakiness, and itchiness. Though no one's sure of its cause, it may be genetic. We do know, however, that heat and sweat often aggravate the condition, which affects 15 percent of all kids, usually before age 5. (About half will outgrow it.) The rash normally appears in skin folds (think elbow and knee creases). It can also show up on the hands, face, and neck.

PREVENT IT: You can't prevent eczema, but you can minimize flare-ups. Avoid fragrances and additives in soaps, lotions, detergents, and dryer sheets (these can irritate skin). Dress your child in cotton clothes to keep him cool, and use an unscented lotion or ointment to keep skin moist.

TREAT IT: Apply a 1 percent hydrocortisone cream for the inflammation. To relieve the itch, try an oral antihistamine such as Benadryl. If the rash recurs or gets worse, call your pediatrician.

Ringworm

Ringworm isn't really a worm—it's an infection caused by a fungus, leading to one or more red, flaky, round or oval-shaped lesions with a raised border. Ringworm is more common in the summer, when fungi grow more rapidly and possibly because children have more skin-to-skin contact with each other then (such as at camp or on the playground). You can also get ringworm from touching infected animals, or objects or surfaces that an infected person or animal has touched.

PREVENT IT: Tell your kid to wash her hands after touching animals and playing sports, and not to share personal items like hairbrushes or clothes.

TREAT IT: Use an over-the-counter (OTC) antifungal cream (like miconazole or clotrimazole). If the lesions persist, see your doctor.

Yeast infection

Candida, the culprit behind most yeast infections, normally lives on our skin and is usually not a problem. But it thrives in warm, humid summer months, upping the chance that it'll trigger an infection in your child. Children in diapers and those on antibiotics (these medications kill the good bacteria that keep yeast in check) are especially prone to yeast infections, which cause a red rash—possibly surrounded by bumps—that itches, burns, or oozes a clear fluid. It usually appears in the skin folds in the diaper area.

PREVENT IT: Change your baby's diapers frequently to reduce diaper rash, which can predispose her to yeast infections.

TREAT IT: Use an OTC antifungal treatment such as miconazole (Fungoid Tincture), clotrimazole (Lotrimin AF), or terbinafine (Lamisil). See a pediatrician if the infection lasts longer than three to five days.

Poisonous plants

Poison ivy, poison oak, and sumac contain urushiol, a resin that can cause a bumpy, blistery, and very itchy rash if you brush up against the leaves of any of these plants.

PREVENT IT: Learn to recognize these pesky plants. Poison ivy is a vine on the East Coast, in the Midwest, and in the South, but it's a shrub-like plant in the North and West. It's most often found near lakes, streams, and trails, but can also grow in your backyard. Poison oak is generally found in the Southeast and on the West Coast. And sumac is a large shrub or small tree that tends to grow in moist areas like marshes and swamps. Best bet: Visit keepkidshealthy.com and do a search for each plant—you'll find photos to help you steer clear. In woods and marshy areas, try to dress your kids in long pants, long sleeves, and shoes that totally cover the feet.

TREAT IT: "Poison ivy often goes away on its own in two weeks," says Krowchuk. But you can relieve symptoms: Give your child a cool-water oatmeal bath and/or apply calamine lotion or a topical ointment such as Caladryl Clear to soothe skin and dry up blisters. If his itching is severe, give him an oral antihistamine. And if it's widespread or severe on his face, head to your pediatrician—your child may need a steroid to control the inflammation.

Heat rash

If your child's arms or torso have suddenly sprouted lots of little red bumps, heat rash—also known as prickly heat—is probably to blame. This rash occurs when skin overheats and sweat gets clogged in pores on the parts of the body where kids (and adults) sweat most.

PREVENT IT: Dress your child in lightweight, breathable fabrics (you can't go wrong with 100 percent cotton) and don't use heavy moisturizers, which can clog sweat glands and trigger a rash.

TREAT IT: Have your child hang out in a cooler, less humid environment when possible, and give her a cool compress or bath if her skin feels warm to the touch. If the redness remains, the rash becomes painful, or the condition doesn't go away in three or four days, call your doctor: These symptoms sometimes signal folliculitis, a bacterial infection of the hair follicles that may require antibiotics.

Your Summer First-aid Kit

Summer lets kids splash and play all day, but those good times also up the chances of getting hurt. "Children are more active in the summer and have less supervision, which may be why we see more accidents," says Martin Eichelberger, M.D., a pediatric trauma surgeon and founder of Safe Kids Worldwide, an organization dedicated to preventing accidental injury to kids. Here's what to do when your child gets hurt.

Cuts, scrapes, and nosebleeds

WHAT TO DO: Using a clean cloth, apply direct pressure to the wound to stop the bleeding. Flush the wound with water to remove any dirt or debris, apply antibiotic ointment, and dress with gauze pads held in place by medical tape—or cover with a plastic bandage. If your child

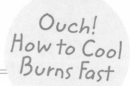
Ouch!
How to Cool
Burns Fast

The sun isn't the only summer scorcher. Outdoor grilling is a major cause of kids' burns, and those ages 5 to 9 suffer the most fireworks-related burn injuries of any age group, according to the National Center for Injury Prevention and Control. Here, pediatricians' top tips for treating burns.

- **SQUELCH THE HEAT.** Immediately run cool water over the burned skin or gently apply a cool compress to reduce the pain. Skip the ice, as the intense cold can make already tender skin hurt even more. If your child's skin is white and leathery, she's suffered a third-degree burn and needs to see a doctor right away.
- **PROTECT THE SKIN.** If the burn is blistering, cover it with sterile gauze while it heals.
- **STEM THE PAIN** with acetaminophen or ibuprofen.
- **CHECK FOR INFECTION.** Burns that seem mild at first but then start oozing or develop red streaks could be infected and should be examined by a doctor.

has a nosebleed, sit her upright and have her tilt her head forward—not back, which could cause her to choke on the blood. Gently but firmly pinch her nose (just under the bony ridge) with a towel for 20 minutes to stop the bleeding. Avoid checking every few minutes to see if the bleeding has stopped; you could dislodge the fresh clot that's forming and cause the bleeding to resume.

WHEN TO SEE A DOCTOR: If there's a deep puncture, don't attempt to clean the wound. Simply wrap it in a clean cloth and call your doctor. Also head to the doctor right away if there are objects deeply embedded in the wound or if the gash is on the foot, since injuries there tend to get infected more easily. Other reasons to seek immediate care: the bleeding does not slow within 15 minutes (the cut may require stitches); the wound shows signs of infection such as swelling or fluid leakage; or the injury has damaged nerves or a tendon (your child cannot move her finger, for example). Also, consult a doctor any time your child has been bitten by an animal.

Banish Boo-boo Fears

"If the sight of blood terrifies your child, use dark washcloths to clean up cuts and scrapes. Better yet, try storing the cloths in plastic bags in the freezer—the coldness will help with pain relief."

Sprains and broken bones

✓ **WHAT TO DO:** If your child broke a bone, he may not be able to move that part of his body without pain. If he *can* move the injured limb or joint, he's probably suffered a sprain or strain, in which case you should wrap the ankle or wrist tightly in an elastic bandage or rolled gauze to compress the swelling. Be careful not to wrap the gauze too tightly, as it may impair circulation. Apply a cold compress to the area—20 minutes on, 20 minutes off—for four to six hours, and elevate the sprain by propping it up on some pillows to stop the swelling and pain. Don't allow your child to walk on the sprain for at least 48 hours; activity can delay healing.

✚ **WHEN TO SEE A DOCTOR:** If your child cannot stand, complains of tingling or numbness, or his foot or ankle is swollen or discolored, he could have a broken bone or a more serious sprain. Keep his weight off the injury and visit the ER immediately.

Head injuries

✓ **WHAT TO DO:** If there's any bleeding, apply direct pressure until it stops. The exception: Avoid putting pressure on her eye. To reduce swelling, alternate 20 minutes on, 20 minutes off, with a cold compress for four to six hours.

✚ **WHEN TO SEE A DOCTOR:** If your child is disoriented, unresponsive, has a headache, can't walk steadily or stand up straight, is vomiting, has neck pain, or has difficulty moving limbs, she could have a concussion or a more serious injury. Go to the doctor immediately if she has any of these symptoms, or is otherwise behaving differently, even if you think the head injury is mild. If she has suffered an eye injury and has decreased vision, pain when moving her eye, or fluid leakage, head to the doctor. And see a doctor or dentist immediately if a permanent tooth—not a baby tooth, which is temporary anyway—was knocked out. If you can find the tooth, rinse it in water, place it in a glass of milk to prevent decay, and bring it with you.

Sex

You don't have to have the birds and bees talk with your young child, but you may need to address his questions about sex sooner than you thought—or sooner than you wanted! Here's how to handle this hot topic.

The Naked Truth: When to Cover Up in Front of Your Child

Your preschooler isn't ready for a sex talk yet, but he is becoming aware of his private parts—and yours. "By the time your child is 3, you should no longer be naked in front of him or her," says Joan Kinlan, M.D., a Washington, D.C.-based child and adolescent psychiatrist. "Many parents feel that being nude around 3- to 5-year-olds will help kids feel comfortable with their own bodies. But it can create sexual feelings in the child, which can be upsetting."

If your child accidentally barges in while you're undressing, don't create a scene. Calmly say, "Oops! You forgot to knock. Please wait until I say you can come in."

As for your kids seeing you in your underwear, experts say that it depends on the parents. "It's important to respect everyone's discomfort with nudity—adult *and* child," says Kinlan.

Let's Talk About Sex

You may be tempted to try what many parents resort to when it comes to talking sex with their kids: avoidance. But that's a bad strategy, says John T. Chirban, Ph.D., author of *What's Love Got to Do With It: Talking with Your Kids about Sex*. "Avoidance tells your child that sex is wrong or silly," he says. Glossing over the truth isn't a great idea either. "In the absence of correct information, kids invent wrong information," says Pepper Schwartz, Ph.D., coauthor of *Ten Talks Parents Must Have with Their Children About Sex and Character.* So you want to be honest—without freaking kids out. The real-mom questions and expert answers here will help you suss out what's too much info for kids, what's not enough, and what's *just* right.

What Makes Daddy . . . Daddy

Well, you know what? A penis does look a lot like a hot dog, especially to a literal-minded toddler. Acknowledge your child's observation ("Sure does, honey"), then give her the right name for it ("That's Daddy's penis") and explain that penises are what boys have—and what girls do not. "Just don't be tempted to describe what a penis is for," says Chirban. "It may only upset or confuse her, and it's not what she was asking anyway." Final note: Always use the proper term when referring to *any* anatomical part. "Sexual body parts are the only ones that we make up cutesy names for, which makes kids feel that there's something embarrassing about them," says Schwartz. "Do you call your elbow a pointy bit? No."

Keep It Short

If your 6-year-old daughter wants to know what a tampon or maxi-pad is for, tell her ("This is for when I menstruate, once a month"), but your honesty doesn't have to extend to a possibly premature biology lesson. It can be upsetting for a child that young to hear about women bleeding from their vaginas. But if she expresses more curiosity about menstruation, says Schwartz, give her the simplest explanation you can ("It's a natural thing a woman's body does to help get ready to have a baby"). And dole out additional information only as she asks more questions—and takes in the answers without looking disgusted or scared, or tuning out. "Remember, your daughter just

"When my then 2½-year-old daughter was showering with her dad, she was right at eye level with his penis. She called it a hot dog and wanted to know why he had one."

"While shopping with my 6-year-old, I picked up some tampons, and she wanted to know what they were for. I tried to give her a brief explanation of menstruation, but I wasn't sure how much info she needed."

needs a page from the book at a time—not the whole book at one go," says Schwartz.

Public Versus Privates

"Unless you're paying big water bills, a little extra penis rinsing is not a problem," says Schwartz. You should neither ignore nor try to stop it—it does feel good, and good for your son for figuring that out. That said, use this as an opportunity to chat about public versus private: "Your penis is a private part, which is why we only touch it in private." And don't worry about explaining the mechanics of erections. If he asks why it gets hard or big, just say, "Yep, that's how they work."

"My son, Jack, 5, loves having his penis rinsed with the handheld shower in the bathtub. Obviously, it feels good. When he gets an erection, should I explain what's going on?"

Answer the Question

"A 7-year-old is going to find sex embarrassing no matter what," says Schwartz. At this age, children are both aware of and repelled by sexuality. The worst thing you can do is to feed the embarrassment by explaining what she saw. Instead, steer yourself back to her question: The best answer is "I was with your dad privately, and sometimes cuddling that way is what we do." It happens; kids sometimes walk in on sex. So don't amp up the anxiety by scolding her. "This situation is about drawing the distinction between privacy, which is a good thing, and secrecy, which isn't," says Chirban.

"My 7-year-old daughter walked in on her father and me having sex recently. Later she said, 'Are you and Dad going to get naked and wrestle again? It's so embarrassing.' I don't want her to find sex embarrassing. What should I have said?"

Honesty Really *Is* the Best Policy

How you answer this mother-of-all sex questions depends on how old your child is when she asks. And, says Chirban, "there are no hard-and-fast rules about the best time to begin a discussion about reproduction." That said, a girl this young may not be asking about reproduction, but rather making a very concrete observation: How does a whole big baby get inside a person? Just to dispel her confusion, it might be a good idea to clue her in to

"Our 5-year-old asked us a bunch of questions about babies and where they come from. When our answers didn't satisfy her, she looked us in the eye and said, 'But how does the baby get inside?'"

Real
Advice
from Real
Moms

Oops, My Kid Saw Us Having Sex—Now What?

"When my 11-year-old walked in on us, she had already had a 'human sexual development' class at school. She said, 'Thank God they didn't show that in the video!' Later, I calmly explained to her the concept of knocking and waiting for the okay before coming into our bedroom. It seems like her seeing us was the best deterrent for early sexual activity—she was totally grossed out!"

how babies, and all living things, start out very small. Try the classic how-a-seed-grows-into-a-plant story—that may satisfy a precocious child's curiosity. But no matter what you say, don't be tempted to rely on easy evasions (ditch the stork, please). "Your child will remember your lie later on," says Schwartz. And while a lie may erode her trust in you, being honest with her will signal to your child that she can come to you with *any* question—now and in the future.

HEALTH

CHAPTER FOUR

Behavior

Whether your child is being tormented by a bully at school or throwing a tantrum at the supermarket, there's an underlying cause—and a solution. Here's the scoop on talking with a bully's mom, stopping your child from teasing his sister, dealing with lies, putting an end to spoiled behavior, and coping with weird kid behaviors like sucking on shirt-sleeves. Check out the ins and outs of kids' behavior—the good, the bad, and often, the very ugly.

Bullying

If your child is being bullied, you have to step in to stop it—but figuring out the right approach isn't always easy. Here's how to handle the bully, as well as his mom, and the helpful things you can say to your child.

How to Stand Up to a Bully's Mom

Her child is making yours miserable, and you want it to stop—*now*. Here, the smart way to get her to talk some sense into her kid.

Step 1 **Don't judge her.**
Maybe you have a pet theory as to how this woman has managed to raise that big bully of hers. Forget all that. "If you go into the conversation with a negative opinion of her—and the attitude that you're a better parent than she is—she'll smell it and won't want to help you," cautions Rosalind Wiseman, author of *Queen Bee Moms & Kingpin Dads: Dealing with the Difficult Parents in Your Child's Life*. The truth is, you don't know a thing about her parenting style or what kind of rapport you two will have, so make no assumptions.

Step 2 **Propose a private conversation.**
You want to minimize public embarrassment here. And it doesn't matter if you phone her or catch her when she's walking past your house. Just say, "Hi, I have something I want to talk to you about. Is this a good time?" If she says, "Sure," but you hear her kid bawling for her, ask to talk later, uninterrupted, for a brief period. Otherwise, you'll rush awkwardly through the talk and nothing will be resolved.

Step 3 **Ask for her help.**

Try, "I've got a problem that I hope you can help me with," says Wiseman; most people are inclined to feel cooperative when you take a we're-on-the-same-side approach. Consider adding, "I'm a little uncomfortable talking to you like this, but I feel it's important." No need to pretend you're cool as a cuke; you're human, and admitting you're anxious makes you easier to relate to.

Step 4 **Give just the facts.**

When you describe the situation, leave out words like "bullying" and "mean." This woman loves her child as much as you love yours, so judgmental language will antagonize her. Instead, just convey the basics, as in: "A month ago, Emma told me that Nicole banned her from the clubhouse the girls use, and started calling her 'stupid' and pushing her away. Emma asked Nicole to stop, but she hasn't. I know Emma may not have told me the whole story, but something's up."

Step 5 **Know what to say if she's receptive . . .**

She may promise to talk to her child and make sure the behavior stops. That's great. Thank her for her time and add, "I hope you'll tell me if my child ever does something you think I'd want to know about." This conveys a feeling of goodwill and makes her kid less of a villain by acknowledging that all children need adult guidance at times.

If she makes a more cautious promise to discuss the matter with her child, that's okay, too. Thank her and tell her you look forward to hearing from her. (If, after a few days, she hasn't gotten back to you—and her child is still being beastly—call her to check in.)

Step 6 **. . . and know what to say if she stonewalls.**

She may think that you're being overprotective or may have trouble admitting that her child ever misbehaves. If so, she's likely to subtly make it sound like you and your child are the problem. She might say, "My, I hadn't heard about this; then again, I don't get involved in every little relationship my

Bluto has." Or, "Kids will be kids, won't they?" Or, "I'm sorry your daughter is upset; she sounds sensitive."

Avoid the urge to go tit for tat and subtly put down *her* child. Says Wiseman: "You'll only be sinking to her level. Plus, it will make her even less likely to cooperate." Instead, say, "We see this differently. That's fine. And I do realize that our kids don't need to be friends. But I know what's upsetting mine, and I'm asking you, as a fellow parent, for help in stopping it." Your firm determination may make an impression on her, even if she doesn't show it. She may rethink things after you leave and may even tell her kid to lay off yours.

Step 7 **Be prepared for a replay.**
Unfortunately, her kid may keep on bullying yours. If so, let the mom know that it's been X number of days, things haven't changed, and you really want her to speak to her child. Then go ahead and pat yourself on the back, says Wiseman, "because you're speaking up for your child—and for decent behavior."

Words to Comfort Your Child

You may not have control over the bully targeting your child, but you do have control over what to say to make him feel better. Here, simple words that will help.

- **"I'M HERE FOR YOU."** A bully makes his target feel friendless, but these words let your child know he's not alone, notes Barbara Coloroso, author of *The Bully, the Bullied, and the Bystander.*

- **"IT'S NOT YOUR FAULT."** You might be tempted to tell your child to toughen up. Don't. You're trying to protect him from hurt, but you're also implying that *your kid* did something wrong. Fact is, only *the bully's* behavior needs to change.

- **"I'D BE UPSET IF THAT HAPPENED TO ME."** The bully wants your child to feel isolated. When he's upset, this type of validation is exactly what he needs to hear.

- **"LET'S SEE WHAT WE CAN DO."** Your child told the bully, "Stop!" and it didn't work. So he'll be relieved to hear you say that he doesn't have to handle the problem all alone anymore.

Our Friends' Kid Is a Bully!

Your friends have a 3-year-old who snatches your 2-year-old daughter's toys away and yanks her around the yard. How can you correct the bully's bad behavior in the presence of her parents without embarrassing—or worse, alienating—mom and dad?

- **CHANGE THE WAY YOU TALK TO YOURSELF ABOUT THE SITUATION—** what psychologists call reframing. Consider viewing your dilemma this way: "Our friends have a 3-year-old who's a spirited little hellion. She's a wild one! My kid gets pushed around by her sometimes, and I'd like to find a way for them to play nice, or at least nicer."

- **STICK WITH DESCRIBING THE KID'S BEHAVIOR**, and keep your own judgment and emotion out of it. Try to refrain from thinking that you can't stand this girl, or that you're going to have to reprimand her; working yourself up like that will just up the odds of your snapping at her, which would, of course, leave her parents displeased.

- **LESSEN THE BULLYING BY INTERACTING WITH THE GIRL IN A FRIENDLY FASHION.** The next time she snatches your child's toy, just step in and say, "Hey, watcha doing? Wasn't Sarah playing with that?" Or, if she's dragging your daughter around, you might try saying, "Whoa, easy there!"

Many parents don't appreciate any outside criticism of their kids whatsoever. So there is a chance you'll upset them, but that doesn't mean you'll lose them as friends. Simply do your best to help the girls work it out—and in the process, you'll model the kind of behavior that will help your daughter grow into someone who can calmly and confidently stand her ground.

Tantrums and Other Unwanted Behaviors

Whether your kid is diving under the table at a restaurant, repeatedly poking his sister, or shrieking at the supermarket because you won't buy his favorite sugary cereal, you need to be prepared to handle all types of unwanted behaviors. Here's your guide to what to do.

Kids Gone Wild!

Is your child biting, throwing tantrums, teasing his sister, or giving you attitude? Hang in there—there *are* solutions. Here, experts share what to do about six real-kid behavior problems.

Teasing siblings

"Most teasing is simply part of the way brothers and sisters engage with each other," says Alec L. Miller, Psy.D., chief of child and adolescent psychology at Montefiore Medical Center/Albert Einstein College of Medicine in Bronx, NY. Siblings tease because they're comfortable enough with each other to say and do things they'd never try out on a friend. "Focus first on the tease-ee," says Miller. Empathize with her, then tell her that the two of you will just ignore the teaser. As for the teaser, try some behavior-modification techniques: He gets a treat if, say, he goes two days without poking his sister. And if you catch him actually being nice to her? "Lavish him with praise," says Miller.

"My 8-year-old son teases his 3-year-old sister. He'll bug her and touch her until she goes nuts, or he takes away her favorite toys."

Tantrums

It could be that your little girl is addicted to the role of drama queen. "Even if you don't indulge her hysterics with concrete rewards—like a candy bar in the supermarket checkout—your negative attention might be encouraging the antics," says Susan Fletcher, Ph.D., a psychologist in Plano, TX. Refuse to accept whining, wailing, or flailing as a form of communication. At home, tell her you'll listen once she calms down, then walk away. If you're in public, remove her from her "audience" and take her outside. Use as few words as possible— "Your behavior is inappropriate and we're leaving the store"—and don't back down. It may take a few tries, but if you're consistent, the next time you threaten to leave, she'll step back, promises Fletcher.

Making messes

Constant yelling about mess help. "That boy is hearing nothing but white noise from his mom at this point," says Miller. Kids are slobs because they can be—and because eventually most parents cave in and clean up for them. Instead, institute a strict system of rewards (a post-soccer-practice sundae when his dirty duds get dumped in the hamper) and consequences (no movie night if they're still on the floor after one warning). "At this age, loss of a privilege has real impact," says Miller. Dial down your house-proud standards for a while, but don't give in. It'll be worth it.

Hateful talk

"When your child says he hates you, he means it—for that moment," says Fletcher. But he does not mean he'll hate you forever; likely, something you've done (telling him "No more cookies") has made him fuming mad. The key is to address what made your child say "I hate you," as opposed to trying to address the fact that he said it. The latter will only have you spinning your wheels as you try to explain how, no, in fact, he does not really hate you. At this age, he doesn't have the reasoning skills to be able to respond, especially when his emotions are running so high. A simple "I guess Mommy made you angry just now, but you still can't have a third cookie" works. When he's calmer, talk to him about how words like "hate" hurt others' feelings.

Dreamy destruction

First, make sure there's no physical reason your daughter's focus seems to have slipped, says Ari Brown, M.D., a pediatrician in Austin TX, and coauthor of *Toddler 411.* Is she getting enough sleep? Could she have a neurological problem? If the change seems very swift or severe, ask your pediatrician for advice. But chances are good that this is just a benign, idiosyncratic—and passing—phase. If no destruction of property is involved, "let her know you don't like what she's doing, but otherwise don't make a big deal out of it," says Miller, because the more fuss you make, the more you might unwittingly prolong the phase. If she is causing damage, bring it to her attention and assign a consequence—helping you clean the dining room chairs is an obvious one. Also, "use her behavior as a reality check," says Miller. "When busy parents are pulled in multiple directions, they may be guilty of paying lots of attention to negative behavior, and little attention to good behavior." So when your daughter does something positive with those markers, like draw a colorful picture, pile on the praise.

"My 7-year-old daughter wanders around doing things without thinking—things she knows not to do, like squeezing a bottle of shampoo into the sink, or writing with a marker on the back of a chair. What can I do?"

Naked at night

Toddlers delight in practicing every new skill they acquire—and the moment they learn how to unfasten diaper tabs, well, it's striptease time! How to deal? "Two words: duct tape," says Brown. You can put duct tape over the diaper tabs, as Brown suggests, or try zip-up sleepers with the extra snap over the zipper, which make it harder for little hands to do their dirty work. You can also give your newly nimble toddler a stuffed animal to diaper and un-diaper to her heart's content.

"My 2-year-old daughter won't stay dressed! She takes off her diaper every night. I find her there in the morning in a wet crib, with her pajamas and diaper in the corner."

How to Handle a Very Public Tantrum

"I leave my groceries, grab my children, and head home. You only have to do this once or twice, and then they'll never have another tantrum."

"I whisper firmly in my son's ear that he cannot make a scene, then redirect his attention by giving him an important task, like putting items in the grocery cart or handing menus to the waitress."

How to Tame Tantrums
(Without Losing Your Cool)

The crying. The kicking. The screaming. A public meltdown can make any parent feel helpless—and humiliated. What to do? Here, four common tantrum-inducing situations, and experts' step-by-step advice on how to cope.

The Supermarket

THE TANTRUM TRIGGERS

- Overstimulation from the bright colors and the overwhelming amount of things to look at and touch
- Seeing things he wants, but knows he can't have
- Boredom

MELTDOWN MANAGEMENT

- **LAY DOWN THE LAW.** Before you go to the store, let your child know what's expected of him. For instance, say, "You can look at the toys, but you aren't going to get any today." He may still beg for that Nemo sippy cup, but he won't be surprised when you don't comply—which makes him less likely to snap.
- **THROW IN SOME FUN.** Keep your child from getting overwhelmed or bored by turning shopping into a game. With toddlers, play peekaboo from behind a box of cereal, make up silly songs, or have them count items as you toss them in your cart. For an older child, give him a part of your grocery list (and a mini-shopping cart if your store has them) and let him find items and cross them off.
- **DON'T SAY NO.** Instead, phrase your no as a yes. When your son asks if he can get out of the cart, say, "Yes, when we get to

the checkout line." You can also avoid saying no by granting half a request. If your little one wants candy, compromise with a healthier treat. Say, "You can't have M&M's, but you *can* have a cereal bar."

The Playdate

THE TANTRUM TRIGGERS

- Frustration over sharing
- A playmate who pushes his buttons
- Losing a game (especially if the winner rubs it in)

MELTDOWN MANAGEMENT

- **TEACH HIM TO LOSE.** It's hard for kids to manage their emotions when things are not going their way. Show your child how to be a good sport by losing a few games when you play with him and letting him see how you respond.
- **DON'T MAKE HIM SHARE *EVERYTHING*.** To alleviate your child's anxiety over sharing, before his friends arrive for a playdate, tell him to put away his favorite toys. Also, let him know that his toys won't be going home with his friend (and make sure they don't!).
- **REFEREE FAIRNESS.** If your child and his pal start battling over a toy, calmly tell them, "We take turns in this house." It's better than saying, "You must share your toys," which doesn't seem as fair to a child. Then count to 15 or set an egg timer to ensure each child gets equal playtime.
- **HELP HIM EXPRESS HIMSELF.** Toddlers get frustrated because they don't have the verbal skills to communicate what they want. Help him make sense of his feelings by verbalizing them, as in "You're upset because *you* want to use that hammer."

Real Advice from Real Moms

How to Handle a Very Public Tantrum

"I deal with it the same way I would at home. Instead of giving in—which would be more convenient for me—I calmly tell my son that we're not moving until he behaves."

"I go around the corner where he can't see me but I can still see him. Once he thinks no one is looking, he settles down."

Prioritize Family Dinner

"I was having problems with my oldest son being rebellious, so I started enforcing family dinner with no TV, no phones, and no guests—just our family. We talk about school, homework, and other concerns the kids might have, and sharing these nightly times together has really improved my son's behavior."

Bedtime

THE TANTRUM TRIGGERS

- Being overtired
- Not wanting to stop an activity
- Wanting more time with you
- Feeling that they're missing out on something by going to sleep (especially if an older sibling stays up longer)

MELTDOWN MANAGEMENT

- **GIVE YOUR UNDIVIDED ATTENTION.** Kids often don't want to sleep because they crave more time with their parents. So despite the cooking, mail, and laundry tasks that await, try to play with your child for at least 15 minutes each evening. And try to involve her in your activities. She can help you fold laundry, or even draw pictures at the kitchen table while you cook.

- **BE PREDICTABLE.** Create a bedtime routine—any combination of bathing, reading, singing, or other low-key rituals—and stick to it. Her ritual will help her brain slow down and prepare for sleep, and a routine takes the blame off of you, making it harder for your child to negotiate to stay up. You can also point to the clock when your child resists sleep: "The clock says we have to stop reading at eight and it's five minutes to eight."

- **GIVE HER A CHOICE.** Getting ready for bed will be easier if your child feels like she's part of the process. But don't just tell her to pick out a book or a stuffed animal to sleep with. Having to choose from so many options will only add to her frustration. Give her two things to choose between instead.

- **SET BACK THE CLOCK.** Your child may be cranky during the day because she needs more sleep. Typically, a 1-year-old needs 14 hours of sleep a day (including naps); a 2-year-old needs 13 hours of sleep; 4- and 5-year-olds, 11 hours; and kids 6 and up, 10 hours. For a child under 4, you can move up her bedtime in one shot. For a kid 4 and up, put her in bed 10 minutes earlier every few days until you hit the right time.

Leaving Someplace Fun

THE TANTRUM TRIGGERS

- Stopping or leaving an activity
- Switching activities, like going from watching *The Wiggles* to getting dressed for school

MELTDOWN MANAGEMENT

- **GIVE HER A HEADS UP.** Being told what to do upsets kids. So make her feel like she's involved in the plan by letting her know exactly when a transition will occur. Say, "When you finish your snack, we're leaving the playground."
- **CREATE RITUALS.** Giving a child a ritual makes her feel like she has some control. It could be a special handshake that she gives her best friend when a playdate is over, or something she always does before leaving the park, such as jumping through the hopscotch squares.
- **TAKE A BREAK.** Between activities, sit quietly with your child on a park bench or in your car for a few minutes so she can decompress. You'll have to plan extra time for it, but it can ward off a tantrum at your next stop.
- **PRAISE HER OFTEN.** When your child doesn't raise a fuss leaving a friend's house, the amusement park, or another activity, acknowledge her good behavior. Kids love positive feedback, and giving them attention for good behavior encourages them to keep it up, no matter what situation they're in.

Real Advice from Real Moms

What Do You Do When Your Child's Idol Makes Headlines for Bad Behavior?

"I tell my kids that these are people who have been given a gift to pursue their dreams, but they forgot that it was a gift and they tossed it away. Then I remind them how important it is to play by the rules and to be honest about who you are."

"When we heard about Jamie Lynn Spears, we sat our 8-year-old down and told her briefly that Jamie Lynn was going to have a baby—but we emphasized that Jamie herself admitted that it was too soon and she's not ready to be a mom. I was glad my daughter heard it from us first and not from her friends at school."

When Nothing Else Works

"We use these moments as an opportunity to talk about the choices you make in life. We asked, 'What choices did that actress have? How will her choices affect her life?' Instead of labeling the person as bad or good, we label the choice. I think this empowers our kids to know that they have the freedom to choose, which makes them much more thoughtful about their actions."

Six steps that will stop a tantrum in its tracks.

1. **MAKE EYE CONTACT.** "Locking eyes helps take kids out of the moment and distracts them so they can calm down," says psychologist Bonnie Maslin, author of *Picking Your Battles*. (Keep in mind, though, that locking eyes when instilling discipline, rather than during a tantrum, isn't a good idea; see page 125.) Also, get down to your child's level to talk—it shows you're focused on listening to her.

2. **WHISPER.** "A child who's screaming can't hear a whisper. Coming close to you to hear you will often switch off their tantrum," says Stella Reid, known as Nanny Stella on the reality television show *Nanny 911*. Using a quiet voice also keeps *you* calm.

3. **PRESS PAUSE.** Sit next to her, gently put your hand on her stomach, and say, "Breathe." This technique forces your child to break from the tantrum, and helps her regroup.

4. **PREVENT AN ACCIDENT.** If your child is doing something that may hurt her or anyone else, wrap your arms around her and hold her firmly but gently until she relaxes.

5. **MAKE A BREAK FOR IT.** "When kids are truly hysterical, there's little you can do except get them out of the place that triggered the tantrum," says New York child psychologist Tovah P. Klein, Ph.D. Scoop them up and calmly say, "This is just so hard for you right now. We'll come back another day." Then escape to a restroom, your car, or a quiet corner to help them mellow out.

6. **IGNORE IT.** If you're at home, don't do anything, says New York City pediatrician Michel Cohen, M.D., author of *The New Basics: A-to-Z Baby and Childcare for the Modern Parent*. The less of a reaction he gets, the less often he'll throw a tantrum.

Weird Kid Behaviors Explained

Children do the strangest, funniest things—and we love them for it. But eating only "white" foods? Diving under restaurant tables? What's up with these odd habits? Here, a guide to understanding—and managing—kids' top worrisome behaviors.

Sucking on shirtsleeves

WHY THEY DO IT: "When kids feel bombarded by sensory input they have no control over, so engaging in behaviors they *do* have control over—like sucking on their sleeves or twirling their hair—calms their anxieties," explains Desmond Kelly, M.D., a developmental-behavioral pediatrician at the Greenville Hospital System Children's Hospital in South Carolina. Plus, oral stimulation is inherently soothing.

HOW TO HANDLE IT: Ignore it. "When parents jump up and down and yell, it tells kids that they're inadequate," says Howard Paul, Ph.D., a professor of psychiatry. "Kids internalize those messages, which can lower their self-esteem and even compound their odd behavior." Instead, try using rewards to encourage him to stop: If he keeps his sleeve dry all day (or even all morning), he gets a sticker on a chart. A weeks' worth of stickers and he can pick a weekend activity.

SEE AN EXPERT IF . . . your child is preoccupied with chewing on his sleeves. He may have what's called Sensory Integration Disorder (SID). With it, a child's five senses fail to properly process and synthesize information from the world around them. (Imagine a cotton shirt feeling like porcupine quills.) Around 15 percent of kids in the United States experience some symptom of SID. If your pediatrician thinks your child has it, she'll likely suggest that he see a pediatric occupational therapist, who will offer coping strategies.

Real Advice from Real Moms

What Do You Do When Your Child's Idol Makes Headlines for Bad Behavior?

"My 6-year-old son heard from friends at school that baseball players Andy Pettitte and Roger Clemens had 'cheated,' so we used it as a teaching moment. We discussed examples of cheating at a game with a friend or in class, and about how it makes others feel."

Cringing at clothing tags

? WHY THEY DO IT: Some kids are sensitive to the feel of textures against their skin. Kelly even knows of parents who turn their kids' socks inside out because the seam at the toe is too irritating.

✓ HOW TO HANDLE IT: "In this case, accommodate the child, because they can't help it," Kelly advises. Kids can build up a tolerance to seams, tags, and itchy fabrics, though, so gradually introduce clothing that's less forgiving. "They can't wear sweatpants all their life," says Kelly.

→ SEE AN EXPERT IF . . . your child can't stand the feel of his clothing and is crippled by sensations most people don't notice—such as the wind on his face.

Putting their hands down their pants

? WHY THEY DO IT: Kids explore "down there" because it's a way to self-soothe, and, because, well, it's pleasurable. "It's really for the same reasons adults do it, only we know to do it in private," says Paul.

✓ HOW TO HANDLE IT: Look at your child's privates to rule out things like a rash. Then think about whether her behavior coincides with stressful events—say, a doctor visit. "When you know what your child is upset by, you can target the anxiety instead of the behavior," says Perri Klass, M.D., professor of pediatrics at New York University and coauthor of *Quirky Kids.* Lessen her anxiety by walking her through a situation beforehand. For an older child, explain what's okay in public and in private. Just don't make it a big deal or make her feel ashamed.

→ SEE AN EXPERT IF . . . the habit interferes with other activities, or if your older child doesn't understand that the behavior should be kept private.

Diving under the table at restaurants

? WHY THEY DO IT: Because they're bored, because it sparks their imagination (It's a cave! It's a submarine!), because they want attention, and/or because they feel anxious and are trying to make their world smaller and more protected.

✅ **HOW TO HANDLE IT**: "If it's boredom or a bid for attention, but they're keeping quiet, let them stay there," says Paul. If they are causing a disturbance, say quietly, "It's time to come out now." If, on the other hand, you think your child is anxious about being in public, try role-playing a restaurant scenario at home. Every day for a few weeks, stage a tea party and ask your child to sit, use good table manners, and chat with you.

➡️ **SEE AN EXPERT IF** . . . your child is so anxious in crowds that it prevents her from doing everyday activities.

Eating only "white" foods

❓ **WHY THEY DO IT**: Maybe your child really can't stand foods with certain tastes, textures, or colors. Or maybe he's exercising his power by eating something different from what you eat.

✅ **HOW TO HANDLE IT**: Once you've ruled out physical causes—such as food allergies or gastrointestinal problems—give him a multivitamin, and buy white foods in the basic food groups (such as cheese, egg whites, or white beans for protein) so that he gets the proper nutrition. Then, says Klass, try banning snacks so he'll be hungry at mealtime, and serve colorful finger foods.

➡️ **SEE AN EXPERT IF** . . . your child isn't gaining weight or if he's anemic. He may have a feeding disorder, which can be a physical and behavioral problem, says Kelly. But don't panic. With this and other odd behaviors, your child is probably just acting his age, and the habit will disappear on its own.

Discipline

Discipline involves much more than screaming at your kids to *stop doing that!* It's a little psychology plus a tone of voice, with a dash of good humor mixed in. Here's the recipe for successful discipline.

Advice from an Expert

Before you say things you might regret in a heated situation, take a few moments to collect your thoughts and count to 10. It really does work to help keep your cool.

Stop Screaming! (Read This Instead)

Imagine getting through an entire day of food fights, tantrums, and misbehavior without losing your cool and shrieking at your children. It *is* possible—and it will help kids learn how to behave better in the long run, claims Hal Edward Runkel, a family therapist, father of two, and author of *ScreamFree Parenting.* Runkel's surprising perspectives on parent-child conflict just might help:

- **REMEMBER WHO'S THE BOSS.** In many families, the children's actions are allowed to determine the parent's reactions and behavior, when it should be the other way around, says Runkel. "Every time you say to your child, 'Don't make me come up there!' or 'Don't make me turn this car around,' you are giving them power over you," he says. "The best thing you can do as a parent is to stay calm and lead by example. Tell yourself, *No matter how childishly they behave, I will always act like an adult.*"

- **EYE CONTACT CAN BE OVERRATED.** Looking your child in the eye when you're exchanging loving glances or reassuring him is fine, says Runkel. "But when you're trying to instill discipline, it can easily turn into a willful staring contest," he says. "Parents may believe they are asserting their place as authorities, but they are actually challenging their child to become defensive." Your kid hears you even if he's not looking at you, so don't escalate the situation—and your own emotionality—by demanding your kid give you eye contact, especially if it hasn't worked in the past. Eye contact often works for tantrums (see above), but not for everyday discipline.

- **KIDS NEED SPACE TO MAKE MISTAKES.** Not every screwup or disagreement is worthy of a showdown, so pick your battles with your child. "Your job as a parent is to help your children grow up and become independent of you," says Runkel, adding that the best way to do this is to give them their own private space—and allow them to make some decisions you might not agree with.

How to Say No (Without Saying No)

The average toddler hears the word "no" an astonishing 400 times a day, according to experts. That's not only tiresome for you but it can also be harmful to your child: According to studies, kids who hear "no" too much have poorer language skills than children whose parents offer more positive feedback. "Plus, saying no can become ineffective when it's overused—a little like crying wolf," says Claire Lerner, director of parenting resources at Zero to Three, a nonprofit that studies infants and toddlers. Some kids simply start to ignore the word; others slip into a red-faced rage the minute that dreaded syllable crosses your lips.

So what's a mom to do—let her child run amok without any limits? "Parents can break out of the yes-no tug-of-war by coming up with new ways to set limits," says Howard Gardner, professor of cognition and education at Harvard University and author of *Multiple Intelligences*. Here, five positive ways to answer your child in the negative.

1. **EXPLAIN YOURSELF AND YOUR FEELINGS.** Consider explaining to your child *why* her behavior—such as banging on the table over and over again— is so bothersome to you. You might tell her, "You're hurting the table when you bang on it, and that makes me sad. Please stop." While it may feel futile to reason with a toddler, you're actually teaching her something: "You're

What Do You Do When You Catch Your Child in a Lie?

"I listen to the lie and then I ask, 'Is that the story you want to stick to?' I tell my kids that they shouldn't lie to parents, because we may be the only ones who can help if they need it."

"When our kids lie, we ask them lots of questions about the details until they eventually trip up. Then we reinforce the fact that lies are very hard to maintain and cause them more trouble than simply telling the truth."

showing your child that what she does affects other people around her—and you're giving her a crash course in empathy," says Leigh Thompson, a professor of dispute resolution at Northwestern University's Kellogg School of Management and a mother of three. "It may take a while for your kid to develop concern for others' feelings, but reminding her of your perspective will help her along," she says.

2. **GIVE HIM A CHOICE.** Your preschooler is throwing his ball in the living room, and you're bracing yourself for the sound of something crashing. Instead of saying, "No! No balls indoors," try saying, "You can roll the ball indoors or take it outside and throw it—your choice." Why? By offering him an option, you help your child feel like he has some power over the situation. Just avoid overwhelming a young child with too many options: For toddlers and preschoolers, two is just right.

3. **SHOW AND TELL.** Three-year-old Henry keeps poking his baby sister; his dad keeps telling him, "No, stop." Why won't he? "Some children can't stop what they're doing, even when you tell them to, because they don't know what to do instead," says parent educator Elizabeth Crary, author of *Without Spanking or Spoiling.* You may have to help them figure it out. Henry, for example, needs his dad to say, "Give Sarah a kiss," or some similar suggestion; then he'll have an image in his mind of something to do instead of poking. Younger toddlers might need you to help them: If your child's hitting the cat, say, "Gentle," while you guide her hand in a stroking motion. Same goes for kids' often irritating habit of kicking and banging—on the table, the back of your seat, whatever. Because she may be doing it unconsciously, help her connect with what her body is doing. You could try a humorous approach: "Tell that foot to stop!" Or simply help her figure out what else she could do with the offending body part: Perhaps your daughter is willing to make quiet little circles with her foot.

4. **SOUND LIKE YOU MEAN IT.** "Kids initially learn the meaning of the word 'no' largely from the tone of your voice when you say it," Lerner says. "So you can communicate what you need to say by using the same firm tone without the negative word." Reserve this strict tone for those times when your child needs to know not to mess with you. Likewise, you can also develop a "look"— or a penetrating glare—that immediately signifies to your child, "I don't like what you're doing, and you'd better stop."

5. **STAY FOCUSED ON THE FUN.** Avoid being a party pooper by helping your child find an activity that's just as much fun as the one you're putting off-limits. If you think your toddler's about to dump a box of cereal on the floor, distract her with something else that's just as entertaining for her, like a favorite toy. "If you stay connected with your child and the fun she's having, she'll be more apt to cooperate with you," says psychologist Lawrence Cohen, Ph.D., author of *Playful Parenting*. And turning her attention—and your own—to something pleasurable will help you relax about the mischief and mishaps yet to come.

The Discipline Trick that *Really* Gets Results

So your kid misbehaved—think you need to dole out the consequences on the spot, as traditional wisdom dictates? Not necessarily, says parenting expert Michele Borba, Ed.D., author of *Nobody Likes Me, Everybody Hates Me*. Sometimes making your kid wait before announcing his punishment can be effective, because the suspense puts him in a bit of distress—a good deterrent to future misdeeds. For a school-age child, you might say: "I want you to think about what you did. After dinner, we'll discuss what to do about it." And with a preschooler, postponing your

Real Advice from Real Moms

What Do You Do When You Catch Your Child in a Lie?

"I tell my 12-year-old daughter, 'You have one chance to tell the truth, and after that you'll be punished'— even after I know she has lied. It works every time and has actually reinforced that telling the truth first is always the best option."

"I tell my 4-year-old that whatever it is she did will not make me as upset as her lying. Then we practice ('If I said my shirt was green, would that be true?') to make sure she understands."

discipline talk for just a few minutes can seem like an eternity—which here, too, gives him time to calm down, think about what he did wrong, and what he might do differently in the future so that he won't get in trouble again. Another benefit to the waiting game: It lets a little guilt set in—which is, after all, the stuff consciences grow on.

Unspoil Your Kids

Okay, so maybe you've given in to your kid's demands once . . . or twice . . . or way too many times. It's not too late to teach him that, like the Rolling Stones, he can't always get what he wants.

Stop the Gimmes

When you're busy and stressed, it's tempting to let your kid eat candy and bread for dinner so you can eat your own fish and veggies in peace. But if your child rarely has to wait between "I want it" and "I have it," then he may be missing out on the chance to develop the emotional tools he'll need to be a happy and successful adult. You *can* put an end to the gimmes—whether it's your child's inflated holiday list or her insistence on treats or snacks as prepayment for good behavior. Here's how to go about implementing the unspoiling process:

Step 1 **Acknowledge where the problem starts.**
As much as we hate to admit it, spoiling is mostly about us parents. "We often try to compensate for what we didn't have as children, to assure ourselves that our children love us, or to make up for any parental guilt we feel," says Diane Ehrensaft, Ph.D., author of *Spoiling Childhood: How Well-Meaning Parents Are Giving Children Too Much—But Not What They Need*. Giving your kids whatever new gizmo they want as soon as they want it is also a way

to show off how successful you are, both financially and as a supermom. Try to figure out where your need to spoil is coming from. Ask yourself a series of questions: Are you tired, overstressed, and trying to find a quick-fix solution? Are you feeling guilty for not spending enough time with your kids? Are you getting more of a kick out of this gift than your child is? Once you figure out what's driving your tendency to spoil your kids, you'll be better able to kick the habit.

Step 2   **Set rules and consequences.**

There is a slippery slope in parenting, where the initial "If you behave, I'll buy you a treat" turns into "Here, take this treat, and hopefully you'll behave." To wean your child off this demand-reward pattern, you'll have to set the new rules in stone. "Observe your child for a few days to notice when she is really being demanding and refusing to take no for an answer," suggests Lisa Forman, a family counselor in Sleepy Hollow, NY. Let's say you recognize a pattern: Your daughter refuses to sit still at the dinner table unless she is promised her favorite dessert. The next step is to come up with a rule and a realistic consequence for her behavior, keeping in mind your child's age and tolerance level. And make sure your partner's on board with the new plan; kids are experts at playing one parent off the other. Then, sit down and explain the rules to your child: "In our house, we get ice cream on Friday night if we have behaved at dinner all week. If there is whining for candy during dinner, you will lose the ice cream privilege." Ask your child to repeat it back to you to make sure she understands—or better yet, make a chart together that she can decorate with stickers each time she follows the rules.

Step 3   **Don't justify your decisions.**

"Parents have this illusion that if they give their children the reason why they can't do what they want, the child will stop wanting it, and as far as I know, that has never happened in the history of parenting!" says Nancy Samalin, a parenting educator and author of *Loving Without Spoiling*. Instead of trying to reason your child into obeying you, simply say, "No, and that's the end of the discussion." If she comes back at you with, "Why?" remind her, "In our house, that is the rule." And as your child repeats her "But why?" refrain over and over, keep this statistic in mind: A survey by the Center for a New American Dream found that kids will ask for something an average of *nine* times before the parents cave. So stay strong and repeat your simple "no" on the ninth, tenth, and eleventh entreaty. Eventually, your child will realize that her attempts are futile, and she'll move on.

Step 4   Resist peer pressure.

When all their other tactics fail, children will inevitably resort to "But all the other kids have one!" Unfortunately, there is no magical response that will definitively shoot this argument down, but there are a couple of strategies that can be successful. "You can say to your child, 'That's interesting. Let's talk about it,'" suggests Ehrensaft. "There may be a good reason for your child wanting what the other kids have: It might be a great new game everyone is playing at recess or a new book they're all talking about. Tell your child that you will look into it, and see if it's something you want him to have." If the book/toy/game seems worthwhile, you can add it to his birthday list—or together you can come up with a strategy for how he can "earn" it, whether that means helping him calculate how much allowance he'll need to buy it (perhaps he needs to save half the price, and you'll kick in the rest) or suggesting it as a reward for a good report card.

Make Meaning, Not Money

There's science behind the saying, "Money doesn't buy happiness." A study from the University of Rochester tracked recent graduates and found that those who achieved goals related to personal growth, relationships, and community were happier than their peers who achieved goals related to fame, money, or image.

Your children know that all they have to do is bat their eyes at *your* mom and that talking Elmo doll is theirs. How to get your parents with the program:

- **SET LIMITS.** One mother of two in Minneapolis said she had present overload after the holidays. "We donated the extra toys to charity, but this year I'm asking the grandparents to buy just three gifts per child: one outfit, one toy, and one book."

- **GET COLLEGIATE.** "Ask your parents to be moderate in their gifts. If they would like to make additional contributions, ask them to consider starting a fund or a trust for your child," says Ehrensaft.

- **REQUEST THE GIFT OF TIME.** Encourage your parents to spend the day with the kids at the botanical garden or baking cookies together, instead of buying them a giant dollhouse or stuffed animal. "Love is spelled T-I-M-E," says Samalin. "Remind your parents that your children love *them*, and not just things they give them."

Step 5 **Brace yourself for the meltdowns.**

The first few times you stick to a new rule and say no, it will be painful—for you, your child, and everyone else within hearing distance. "There will be meltdowns at first, so fasten your seat belt and react to them in a very calm and neutral way," suggests Ehrensaft. "If you hold to that line every day, your child will learn that this is not the way to get something that he wants, and he will eventually stop." In fact, experts compare this part of the de-spoiling process to sleep-training your baby: a week or so of stress and tears, and then one blissful night your baby sleeps till morning—or your kid finally understands the word *no*.

Step 6 **Share the thrill of anticipation.**

While our instant-gratification culture has made life easier in many ways, it has also diluted the joy of looking forward to special experiences. "When kids are accustomed to getting things right away, nothing excites them anymore," says Steven Friedfeld, a family therapist in New York City. "The bar has been raised so high that by the time they're teenagers, they might start looking toward other things—like alcohol and sex—for thrills." Friedfeld also points out that teaching your children to wait for fun and treats helps them sustain focus and attention, two very important skills for success in school. One of the best ways to teach anticipation is to give your child an allowance and let him save it toward the item he covets. Other parents have found wish lists to be a powerful tool. Make the list finite: She can keep 10 items on it at any given time; to add a new wish, she has to eliminate an old one. This not only helps her prioritize what she truly desires but also shows your child that a toy she swore she couldn't live without in April may seem less important in July.

Step 7 **Indulge in nonmaterial joys.**

By now, your child should be behaving so wonderfully that you will be tempted to smother him with tons of treats. Luckily, there are plenty of things you can bestow in abundance without running the risk of spoiling: snuggling on the couch and reading books; saying "I love you"; popping a bowl of popcorn and watching the football game; listening to her tell an elaborate story about a princess and her magical purple rhinoceros without even once checking your cell phone. And don't forget those weekly rewards for good behavior—if your child has followed all the rules you set, go ahead and share an ice cream sundae or do each other's nails. Because when you strip the parent-child relationship down to its core, it's pretty simple: Most kids would forgo another stuffed animal in favor of time with you. And that's something money can't buy.

CHAPTER FIVE

Emotional Life

Anger, sadness, fear, envy: When your child is overcome with intense emotions, you *both* feel it. Fortunately, there are practical steps you can take to help your son cope with troublesome feelings or to help your daughter celebrate her happiness and first love. Here's how to guide your child to understand, deal with, and feel good about his feelings.

Feelings

Feelings—both good and bad—can be overwhelming at times, especially for kids who don't yet know how to cope with them. Read on and learn the secrets to helping your little one corral those feelings—and grow stronger in the process.

Help Kids Feel Good about Their Feelings

You help your child develop his brain and hone his physical skills, but what about his emotions? Teaching him how to deal with his own feelings—rather than get caught up in them—is one of the most critical life skills you can impart. Here's how to give your child the tools he needs to work through his emotions—now and into adulthood.

- **EASING ANGER.** For a little kid, heart-pounding, lump-in-the-throat anger can be so overpowering that the only way to cope is by lashing out. That's just what happened to the daughter of Victoria Manion Fleming, Ph.D., an educational psychologist and executive director at North Shore Wellness Services in Northbrook, IL. Her 5-year-old became so angry when her younger sister broke one of her Happy Meal toys that she started screaming and crying at the top of her lungs. To help her 5-year-old cool off, Fleming got down to her daughter's eye level, held her hands, and told her to breathe slowly. "Once she was calmer, I helped her list what she was feeling," says Fleming. "You're mad your sister took the toy without asking. You're mad that she broke it. And you're *really* mad because she doesn't care that she broke it." Listing feelings in simple terms helps kids unravel the anger to its root cause and makes

Get Feelings Out There, Good *and* Bad

"When I had a cranky child on my hands, I'd swoop her into my lap and say, 'It's time to complain, so let's complain together. Oh, I feel so angry, or hurt, or sad,' hugging her the whole time and letting her be cranky. After a while, she felt soothed and ready to move on. Also, she learned to put words to her feelings."

Real Advice from Real Moms

How Do You Get Your Child to Open Up and Tell You About Her Day?

"I go through my daughter's backpack, and as I pull out each piece of art or schoolwork, I ask her about it. It's as if she's picturing being at school and remembering all the details."

"I try to think of something funny or weird that happened in my day, and that sometimes spurs on a story from my kids. Sharing how silly I can be makes them want to share too."

it manageable. The 5-year-old was able to resolve her anger by telling her sister just how bad she felt.

- **LIFTING SADNESS.** When 8-year-old Hunter was told that his family was moving from Ohio to Georgia, "he put his head down on the table and just sobbed," says his mom, Melanie. "He was upset for days." Like most parents in the same situation, Melanie just wanted to make the hurt go away, pronto. Not a good idea, warns Fleming: "You have to let *him* decide when he's ready to look on the bright side." Rushing your child to "feel better" sends the message that you're uncomfortable with his sadness, and by extension, that there's something wrong with him. Instead, talk through what's making him sad. Say, "Let's get some ice cream, and then we can talk more about what's bugging you." Eventually, you can encourage your child to "do something" about his sadness. In Hunter's case, "we went online to find fun things to do in our new town," says Melanie. (A word of caution if you're the mom of a boy: Let him show vulnerability. "We limit the development of empathy in boys when we tell them that they shouldn't cry," says Mary Polce-Lynch, Ph.D., a developmental psychologist in Ashland, VA, and author of *Boy Talk: How You Can Help Your Son Express His Emotions*.)

- **CELEBRATING HAPPINESS.** What's the matter with kids feeling happy, you ask? Nothing at all. But "just as with other emotions, your child may need help channeling his glee appropriately," says Fleming. Kids can get so exuberant that they scream, run around, and act out of control, which might be fine at home, but not at, say, the library or Grandma's house during a quiet dinner. When that happens, take your child aside without making a scene, and tell him that you're happy for him, but that it's time to calm down and read a book or draw. Just don't chide him. "You don't want him to connect his feelings with shame or embarrassment," says Polce-Lynch.

EMOTIONAL LIFE

Sometimes kids can't help but gloat. If your child wins a game, he's entitled to do the happy dance, but not to make others feel like losers. "Joy isn't bad; insensitivity is," says Fleming. "When a joyful, look-at-me celebration hurts someone, it should be pointed out." Say, "It's great that you scored the winning goal; now let's congratulate the other team's goalie on the great job he did."

Moving Time: Helping Kids Say Good-bye

The end of the school year is often the start of moving season, as families use the summer break to house-hunt and pack up the moving van. If your child's best friend is moving away, the loss can feel big, and the child may mourn for months, says Raymond Crowel, a vice president at the National Mental Health Association. Let him know that it's okay to feel sad and talk about his feelings, and don't nudge him into new social situations too soon. "Trying to push him into new friendships makes light of the relationship he lost," Crowel says, and has the paradoxical effect of making the mourning process take longer. Instead, encourage your child to e-mail, instant message, or call his friend to keep in touch. Some kids will simply want to spend a little time on their own for a while, Crowel says. It's okay to let them do so: "You want to let them heal themselves," he says.

Real Advice from Real Moms

How Do You Get Your Child to Open Up and Tell You About Her Day?

"I'll mention a specific kid and ask my daughter Serena what they did that day together, or what she did at 'choice time.' Once we get the conversation started, she usually opens up and tells me lots of other things on her own!"

"We play a game called Sunshine/Cloud. At dinner, everyone takes turns telling the worst part of their day—their cloud—and then the best part of the day— the sunshine! Not only do the kids open up, they also listen to you. My son has even given me very sweet advice when I talk about my cloud."

Depression

You may think depression strikes only adults—but in fact, it's a very real and growing problem for kids. Determining if your child is just going through a moody phase or if she is depressed is tough. Here's how to identify depression in your child, and what to do about it.

Is it Moodiness . . . or More?

It's more than just the blues: Clinical depression among kids is on the rise. In fact, depression is the second most common childhood mental health problem. (Attention deficit/hyperactivity disorder is number one.) Less than a fourth of the estimated 12 million kids in the United States who suffer from psychiatric disorders receive treatment, however, which places them at high risk for failing school, abusing drugs and alcohol, and committing crimes. Kids with untreated depression also are 12 times more likely to commit suicide.

Even though up to 80 percent of depressed kids improve with treatment, many parents delay seeking help because of the stigma of mental illness. Other parents hope their child will get over it on their own. But "depressed kids aren't just going through phases that they'll outgrow—they find it difficult to manage their emotions without professional help," says child psychiatrist Harold Koplewicz, M.D., founder of the New York University Child Study Center.

Figuring out the difference between true depression and temporary moodiness is crucial. Here's how to tell if your child has a problem—and what you can do to help.

What are the warning signs?

While all children feel sad from time to time or have the occasional bad day, a child with depression remains in a funk for weeks or months. During this time, she's likely to struggle at school, isolate herself from friends, cause problems at home, and act angry, moody, and irritable. Depressed kids are also as confused by their emotions as their parents are; they can't describe how they're feeling. Instead, they might complain about stomachaches, develop exaggerated fears, grumble about being bored, lack energy, or talk about death.

Why do some kids suffer?

Though experts still aren't sure why certain children are more likely to become depressed, the following factors may play a role:

- **THEY'RE BORN WITH A "BLUE GENE."** There's a 25 percent chance a child will struggle with depression if one parent has it; that risk jumps to 50 percent or more if both parents are affected.
- **THEY HAVE A CHEMICAL IMBALANCE.** Chemicals in the brain called neurotransmitters—namely serotonin, norepinephrine, and dopamine—play a vital role in regulating emotions. Experts think that depressed kids may not produce enough of these chemicals.
- **THEY'RE DEALING WITH TRAUMA.** Up to half of all depressive episodes (among kids *and* adults) are preceded by life-altering events. Losing a loved one, dealing with a parental divorce, moving to a new home, or being the victim of abuse can be particularly traumatic to kids who haven't yet developed coping skills.
- **THEIR HORMONES ARE IN FLUX.** Kids as young as preschool age can have depression, but the disorder is most likely to be diagnosed around puberty, when hormones kick in. Boys and girls are equally at risk for depression until puberty; during the teen years and throughout adulthood, females are up to

Real Advice from Real Moms

How Do You Turn A Frown Upside Down?

"One thing that turns my kid's bad moods around is a bath—especially with bubbles or lots of toys. There's something about that nice warm water that always gets them smiling again."

"Whenever one of my four kids gets grumpy, I just start laughing. I have a really strange, wheezy laugh, and it always makes them crack up. I can tell that it's working when my oldest starts to snort!"

"I tell my daughter that we can pull out the bed from the sofa and watch television and eat lunch on it. She thinks it's the coolest thing that a bed pops out from under the sofa, and that makes her forget whatever she was grumpy about."

two times as likely to be depressed. Fluctuating hormones, as well as differences in societal expectations, likely account for this gender bias. "Girls are encouraged to express their emotions, while boys learn to bottle them up," says Koplewicz. As a result, depression in girls may often be easier to recognize.

How can you get help?

Even if a child's dark cloud lifts, research shows there's a 60 percent chance she'll be depressed again unless she gets treatment, and her lifetime risk for depression goes up with each untreated episode. First, talk to your child's pediatrician; if she suspects a problem, she'll likely refer you to a mental health specialist, such as a child psychiatrist. If depression is diagnosed, the following treatments can help:

- **PSYCHOTHERAPY.** Kids with mild depression often respond well to talking about their problems with a mental health professional, who helps them identify and change negative patterns of thinking.

- **MEDICATIONS.** Antidepressants, namely selective serotonin reuptake inhibitors (SSRIs) such as Prozac (the only medication FDA-approved to treat depression in kids), can greatly alleviate symptoms in children by elevating brain chemicals. Despite this, pediatric prescriptions for SSRIs have declined nearly 25 percent since 2004, when the FDA issued a warning that their use may induce suicidal thoughts in youths. "Overall, depressed kids see significant improvements with SSRIs. But because every child responds differently, kids starting these medications should be closely monitored," says David Fassler, M.D., author of *Help Me, I'm Sad: Recognizing, Treating, and Preventing Childhood and Adolescent Depression.* A large study found that the benefits of giving antidepressants to kids outweigh the risks.

EMOTIONAL LIFE

● **COMBINED TREATMENT.** Depressed kids improve the most when they take medications *and* participate in psychotherapy. Nearly three out of four children on combined treatment reported that their depression lifted, while 61 percent improved with medication alone and about a third got better with only psychotherapy.

To learn more about childhood depression and to find a mental health professional in your area, visit Families for Depression Awareness at familyaware.org

Signs Your Child Is Depressed

Is your child:

- irritable, angry, or cranky for no good reason?

- uninterested in spending time with friends or participating in fun activities?

- experiencing frequent stomach or head pains?

- losing weight?

- sleeping more than usual?

- doing poorly in school?

- talking about running away from home?

- lacking energy or complaining a lot about being bored or tired?

- suffering from low self-esteem?

- talking about hurting or killing herself?

- giving away favorite belongings?

If you answered yes to five or more of these questions and your child has displayed these behaviors for at least two consecutive weeks, she may be clinically depressed.

Love

Love is a many-splendored thing, especially when it's a first crush. But puppy love can also be tricky. Here's the right way to handle it.

Happiness Is Contagious

It turns out that there might be something behind coming down with a case of the giggles. Research from Harvard Medical School has determined that happiness is emotionally contagious to up to three degrees—meaning your good mood can spread not only to your kids, but to their friends and their friend's friends, too. Share a smile with one of these bonding rituals and launch a joy epidemic!

Move it, move it!

"We dance around the living room to one of my older son's favorite tunes—'Don't Worry, Be Happy,' or anything by Chuck Berry. While my husband and I dance on the rug, our older son likes to jump off the couch and do spins. The 2-year-old shimmies his hips and has a few jazz moves. Our evening dance party takes me right out of my world of work and clients and into the world of laughter and music with all of my boys."

Share the love.

"During dinner we share one thing that we love about each other. Recently, my youngest daughter said to me, 'Mom, I love how you live in the moment and how you always take care of me and listen to me.' I said to her, 'I love how sensitive you are, how easily you talk about your feelings, and how you're so grateful for everything I do for you. You always say thank you and that makes me feel really good inside.' Everyone takes a turn, and by the end of all our affirmations, we each feel loved, appreciated, and connected."

Backwards night.

"Every now and then, we have 'backward night.' We skip homework (putting it off until the next morning), put on our pj's, and play board games until my husband comes home from work. For dinner, we have pancakes, scrambled eggs, sausage, and orange juice. Afterward we grab blankets, snuggle on the sofa, and watch DVDs. It gives us all a chance to let go of the rules for a short period of time and relax together. It also creates really great family memories."

Your Child's First Crush

Has your child found a special someone? "Childhood crushes can start as early as age 3 or 4," says Elyse Goldstein, Ph.D., a psychologist in New York who specializes in relationships. "It's a normal step toward independence." So what should you do if your daughter says she's in love with a boy in class?

- "Reinforce her enthusiasm and encourage her to talk about her crush," says Goldstein. "You're teaching your child how to open up and share herself with another person."
- Ask lots of open-ended questions about what your child likes most about her crush.
- Don't ever belittle her feelings. "Your child takes her crush very seriously," says Goldstein. "If you make fun of it, she'll think that there is something wrong with liking another person."
- Finally, don't forget that it's called a *crush* for a reason: Your child will go through some heartbreaks. Make sure she knows that while rejection can be tough, that's no reason to shy away from love.

Fears

Kids have reasonable fears, and sometimes have irrational fears—and they're all very real. Where do these fears come from, and how can you help your child deal with them? Here's what you need to know.

The Fear Factor

Being scared of a specific thing or situation is actually normal in kids—in fact, we humans are hardwired to be afraid as a means of survival. There's a reason that stranger anxiety, for example, crops up in infants around 7- to 9-months-old: It helps them maintain a close proximity to their parents, which is necessary for them to thrive.

Besides the innate fear they're born with, kids also learn caution from their parents. You tell your daughter not to play with matches; as a result, she may become afraid of fire. Preschoolers also pick up fears from specific events. After your son watches *Shark Tale,* he might suddenly be afraid to get in the pool with you. Experts say these fears are a normal and natural part of growing up. Your child should outgrow them in a few months.

And then there are the fears that seem to come out of nowhere, of birds, say, or of the vacuum cleaner. These are often more challenging—and perplexing—to parents. Yet even these out-of-the-blue fears are completely normal, and most children also get over this type of fear within a few months. In the meantime, there are things you can do to reassure your child and help him shed his anxiety more quickly.

- **DON'T BRUSH OFF YOUR CHILD'S EMOTIONS.** "I often hear parents say, 'Why is my child acting so afraid? It doesn't make sense,'" says Fred Penzel, Ph.D., a psychologist and executive director of Western Suffolk Psychological Services in Huntington, NY. "They try to minimize the situation by telling the child that his fear is nothing to worry about. That strategy usually backfires," he says.

- **BUT DO USE A MATTER-OF-FACT TONE.** Acknowledging the fear is important, but "you don't want to go in the opposite direction and excessively reassure your child," says Alexandra Barzvi, Ph.D., clinical director for the Institute of Anxiety and Mood Disorders at the New York University Child Study Center. "That sends the message that there *is* something to be afraid of."

- **TALK IT OUT.** That's what Christina Lerman of Brooklyn did after her 8-year-old daughter announced she didn't want to go on a family trip to Disney World. "I asked her why and she brought up the spinning teacup rides she'd seen at amusement parks," says Lerman. "She is afraid of people throwing up, and I realized she was terrified that they were going to be puking everywhere at Disney World because of the rides." Lerman and her husband explained that Disney isn't like ordinary amusement parks—it has more theme rides than thrill rides. "And we told her that thousands of visitors go there every year. If everyone kept throwing up no one would go back!" Lerman says. By countering her daughter's misconceptions with concrete reasons why the worst wouldn't happen, Lerman dispelled her fear.

- **HELP YOUR CHILD CONFRONT HIS FEARS.** It's also critical that you not allow your child to avoid what scares him. "One thing we know for sure is that avoidance fuels fear," says Barzvi, "and the next time your child is faced with the same anxiety-provoking situation, he will remember he wasn't able to cope with it last time." To prevent your child's anxiety from becoming overblown, gradually bring him into more contact with the object of his fears. If your son is afraid of doctors, first read him an age-appropriate book about doctors. Then buy him a doctor's kit so he can play doctor on his own. Finally, visit your pediatrician's office one afternoon just to meet the assistants and nurses. After your child accomplishes each new

Soothing Fears

Whether your child's fear is rational (being dunked in water or bitten by a dog) or fantastical (monsters under the bed), respect them. After all, your child's fears are *all* real to her.

"When my daughter was 3, she loved playing in the water. So I was surprised when she said one morning that she was skipping swim class. She told me she didn't feel well, but when I pressed her, she said, 'I'm afraid the teacher is going to drop me under water.' I said that, together, we'd tell the swim teacher not to drop her. She felt better instantly, popped into her suit, and off we went."

step, praise him for doing such a good job. Also, you can help a child better deal on her own by arming her with coping skills. Teach your daughter to take deep breaths when she sees a bug or to keep a flashlight by her bed to make nighttime less scary.

● **BE A GOOD ROLE MODEL.** Your children will always look to you first for behavior cues. Is your daughter afraid of dogs? Even if you're afraid too, try to smile and pet friendly dogs in the neighborhood. She'll be less likely to pick up on any apprehension you may have.

If you find that your child's fears don't go away after a few months or that they intensify, see your pediatrician, who may refer you to a behavioral therapist.

When Fears Become Phobias

If your child's distress begins to keep her from taking part in everyday life, and she obsesses about it, her fear may have escalated to a phobia—defined as a fixed, overgrown, unrealistic fear. Early signs include being clingy, tearful, or oppositional when around the fear. An example of a phobia: Your child doesn't just hate the sight of bugs, but dreads leaving the house because she's afraid she might see one. "That's when you need to talk to your pediatrician about getting behavioral therapy," says Barzvi. "This extreme fear puts stress on your child and may not go away on its own. Left untreated, a child's school performance may drop, her relationships with friends may become strained, and her self-esteem could be affected." The most successful treatment is a combination of cognitive behavioral therapy, which draws out from your child what scares her and why, and behavior therapy, which slowly helps your child face her fears. First, she and the counselor may talk about what it is about bugs she doesn't like. Then they'll look at picture books about bugs together, then play with an ant farm, and finally actually even collect bugs. Although there's really no way to prevent your child from developing a phobia, if you recognize one early on, you can usually eliminate it or reduce its intensity after a few months of therapy.

Envy

Has this green-eyed monster invaded your house? If envy is getting the best of your child, you can take the practical steps below to help him push it away.

Keep Envy from Eating at Your Kids

Kids can experience envy—over someone else's looks, skills, popularity, possessions, you name it—as early as preschool, and teaching them how to handle it is more important than you may think. "If kids constantly envy their siblings or peers, they start to feel bad about themselves by comparison, which can pummel their self-esteem and even lead to depression," says Michele Borba, Ed.D., parenting educator and author of *12 Simple Secrets Real Moms Know*. Here's how to help your child keep jealousy at bay, and do damage control when envy rears its ugly head.

- **NOTICE THE SIGNS, AND SYMPATHIZE.** It can be hard for kids to recognize—let alone deal with—their own emotions. So be on the lookout for signs of envy, which include external signals, such as hitting, teasing, or criticizing the person they envy ("You're such a show-off!"), and internal ones, such as stomachaches, sadness, anxiety, withdrawal, or lack of motivation ("There's no point in even *trying* to play when he's so much better than me."). Then verbalize the feeling: If while your 5-year-old is doing cartwheels and the grandparents are clapping, your 3-year-old looks on the verge of tears, say, "Boy, your sister's getting all the attention! That's not so great, is it?" If she agrees, give the feeling a name. "I can see how that might make you *jealous,* and that's okay." That understanding alone can make her feel better. "What children need most is simply for you to listen and validate their feelings," says Keith Crnic, Ph.D., a psychology professor at Arizona State University in Tempe.

- **SHOW *YOUR* JEALOUS SIDE.** It's reassuring for kids to hear that someone they respect has battled similar demons. "Sharing stories of when you've felt jealous can show your child how to get to the bottom of why he's feeling a certain way and handle it," says Borba. When 9-year-old Zak complained about not being able to go to ski club like his older brother, his mom, Kristi, of Cleveland, told him, "I wasn't allowed to cross the street by myself till I was 12, but my younger sister got to visit Siberia when she was 14—can you believe it?" The story got Zak's mind off of being upset, and gave him a lesson in managing his envy. "I told him I learned to accept that things aren't always going to be the same for each child," his mom says.

- **DON'T "GO NEGATIVE."** "Kids learn to regulate their emotions in part by watching how their parents behave," says Crnic. So when you sense jealousy rising in your child, don't get defensive on her behalf, place blame, or reject the other person—all of which incite her to take disappointment personally (a major root of envy) and make her feel worse. Be positive and do what Janne Kaminski of Montclair, NJ, did when her 4-year-old daughter found out that she had not been invited to a party. "That's okay," Kaminski said, matter-of-factly. "Everybody has different friends." Her explanation helped her daughter understand why she wasn't invited without making her feel bad for being left out.

- **FIND A PRACTICAL SOLUTION.** With envy, kids are just wishing," says Borba. "But if they take control of the situation, they'll feel that they can help themselves, which boosts their self-esteem and winnows down jealousy." For example, if your child feels that other kids on his baseball team always get to play more than he does, ask him, "Do you think it might help if you practiced more?" He'll see that although he can't control the coach's choices, he *can* control his response—by improving his game and increasing the chance he'll get to play.

- **WATCH THE COMPARISONS.** You may not realize it, but even saying "Sally is so pretty!" or smirking, shrugging, or raising an eyebrow when talking about your child's peers or siblings can be interpreted as a comparison.

These steps will help tame your child's jealousy over others' possessions.

- **LAY DOWN HOUSE RULES.** Talk to your child about your values, and set rules on what family members can and cannot buy based on those values—such as no violent video games, or no toys that cost more than a certain amount of money. Knowing that each family has different rules helps your child accept that she won't always have the same stuff as her friends.

- **PUT HIM IN CHARGE.** Letting your child choose what to buy with his own money—whether it's an allowance or his piggy-bank savings—helps him manage his expectations and forces him to really think about what he wants or needs. "Next time they envy another child's toy, they'll realize: I made choices about what to buy and I chose to buy different toys," says Crnic. Even very young kids can learn to save for a purchase, and those 6 and older are ready for an allowance.

- **KEEP A WISH LIST.** When your child asks for a toy, have her add it to a list that you'll consult before birthdays or holidays. It satisfies her immediate need to be heard, and the potential of getting what she wants will make her less jealous of those who have the toy.

And "if your child doesn't measure up in some area, she could envy kids who do," says Borba. Christine Hierlmaier Nelson of Foreston, MN, once told friends that she didn't want to cut her 2-year-old daughter's hair because it was so curly, and that her older daughter, 5, had never had curls. She knew she'd screwed up when her older daughter asked to have her hair curled with a curling iron. "Ever since then, I've consciously complimented her hair," Nelson says.

● **GIVE AN EXPLANATION.** With material wants, explain why your child can't have what she covets—for instance, "You're not big enough for a skateboard yet"—says Thomas Chiaromonte, Ph.D., a professor of child development at Fullerton College in California. Having a rationale is often enough to get kids over their jealousy, and they'll learn to weigh their desires against what's reasonable as they grow up.

● **HELP KIDS DISCOVER THEIR OWN SPECIAL GIFTS.** "Kids with low confidence tend to accentuate their weaknesses, and that feeling of inadequacy can make them more apt to be jealous of others," says Crnic. "So parents need to build kids up." Let your child know that you like and are proud of who he is, and nurture his strengths. If your son's a budding Picasso, take a real interest in his paintings. When he solves a problem—anything from a stuck zipper to a math equation—say you're proud of him. "If kids feel good about who they are, they'll find it easier to see others getting attention for who *they* are," says Crnic. That confidence not only helps your child cope with envy, it encourages him to be himself—a truly enviable skill.

CHAPTER SIX

School
(and Other Ways of Learning)

As your child inches (or storms) toward his school years, you begin to realize that there's a lot more to school and learning than picking out a really cool lunch box. How can you best help with your child's homework—or should you help at all? What after-school activities are right for your child? Should you banish computer games—or can they be worthwhile? How can you prepare your kids for going back to school in September—and prepare yourself for the inevitable onslaught of forms? Here are the answers to your questions, and lots of ways to keep school stress at bay.

Teachers

Your child's teacher is a critical link in his growth—she might even change your kid's life! To help her nurture your child's development—and thank her for her hard work—read on.

5 Things Your Kid's Teacher Needs from You

The best way to ensure your child has a successful school year? Cultivate a positive relationship with her teacher. There are five core values that will make or break that bond. Here's how to understand and maximize them.

1. **ENGAGEMENT.** It may sound obvious, but participating in your kid's education, even minimally, can do wonders. "Children whose parents are involved with their education generally tend to be less disruptive in class," says Reg Weaver, former president of the National Education Association.

   How engaged should you be? First and foremost, be sure that your child makes homework a daily priority—over sports and clubs. Also, don't skip the school's open house, even if it's your kid's third or fourth year there. Another great way to make an impact is to attend a few PTA meetings. Too busy for the PTA? Ask the teacher if there's something she can use, such as tissues, pencils, erasers, or crayons.

2. **TRUST.** Teachers have a deep appreciation for parents who really listen to their opinions and consider their expertise, especially when it comes to bad news. If the teacher's telling you something about your kid that's upsetting, keep your cool. Don't call the principal; it shows that you don't trust the teacher. In fact,

Real Advice from Real Moms

How I Save $$$ on Teacher Gifts

Want to show appreciation for your kids' teachers—without taking out a second mortgage to cover them all? These low-cost ideas have a personal touch.

"This year, my boys (ages 5 and 6) and I are making bracelets. I picked up some charms with each teacher's first name on them, and I've had my kids help select the beads and colors. They've done a really great job!"

"One year, all the parents chipped in to get a few large clay pots and had the kids in the class put their handprints on them with paint. Then we gave the teacher a gift certificate to Lowe's so she could buy plants to put in the pots."

"Coming from a family of teachers, the one gift that I know all teachers appreciate most is a letter stating how much they touched your child's life, or how impressed you are with what your child has learned, or even a simple thank-you. Teachers usually become teachers for a reason. A letter like this reminds them they made the right choice."

Kennon McDonough, a school consultant to San Francisco Bay Area preschools, recommends actually thanking the teacher for sharing upsetting news. And even if you don't ultimately agree with the teacher's opinion, you'll have increased her trust in you simply by listening and considering what she's shared with you.

3. **COMMUNICATION.** Communication about your kid's health, happiness, and progress needs to flow both ways. "If there's an illness or a crisis going on, your child's teacher needs to know about it because it may explain why your child isn't behaving well or performing academically," says McDonough. You can share positive developments, too. "The more you can paint a true and full picture of who your child is, the more it helps the teacher," McDonough says. E-mail is a great way to bridge home and school.

4. **APPRECIATION.** "Kids can't show gratitude toward their teacher every day, so it's important for parents to do it," McDonough says. But that doesn't mean you have to buy extravagant gifts. "Whether a parent leaves a muffin, a flower, or a note on my desk, it makes my day," says Nancy Martin, a preschool teacher in San Mateo, CA. At the end of every school year, Merritt Rowe, a Nashville mother of three, writes a long note thanking her kids' teachers for all they did. "I know it means a lot to the teacher," she says.

5. **RESPECT.** Teachers' number one request of 21st-century parents: Get off your cell phone to say hello to the teacher when you pick up your kid. Another frequent faux pas? Dropping your kid off at school late. "You need to get your child to school on time," says Jo Ann Brooks, a preschool teacher in Richmond, VA. Likewise, be sure to return forms like permission slips within 24 to 48 hours of receiving them; your child may forget about them, so check her backpack daily. If you forget, just apologize. "Teachers hear excuses from kids all day long," McDonough says. "They don't need to hear them from parents, too."

SCHOOL

Homework

Homework doesn't have to be a hassle—if both you and your child know how to handle it. Here's advice from researchers and moms on making the most of those after-school assignments.

What *Really* Helps Kids Get Better Grades

The best way for parents to help kids who do poorly in school? Back off, say researchers at the University of Illinois at Urbana-Champaign. When moms and dads nagged kids about homework, grades dropped. But when they fostered independence by helping kids come up with solutions, grades improved. Here's what to do:

- When your child is doing his homework, don't pull up a chair and join him. Be around, but don't add pressure by watching him.
- Don't offer guidance unless he asks for it. And never do work for him. It will make him lose focus—and confidence. If he's not doing the work, set a better time for it—or set consequences—together.
- If he makes a mistake, don't be tempted to correct it. Help him find solutions by asking questions. Instead of saying, "Come on, you know eight times seven is 56," ask, "What's eight times seven again?"

Real Advice from Real Moms

How Do You Get Your Kids to Do Homework Without Nagging?

"Every day the kids do their homework, they get a star. If they get stars for every day of the week, then we do something special on Friday, like pizza or ice cream."

Reading and Rhyming

Take your child's ABCs to a whole new level with silly voices and creative rhymes. Try the strategies below to make the reading experience even more fun for both of you.

When You're Tired of the Same Old Story

Why do your kids never tire of hearing the same tale again and again? "Kids learn through repetition," explains Susan B. Neuman, Ph.D., a professor of educational studies at the University of Michigan and the author of *Reading to Your Young Child.* "Reading the same story over and over helps them focus on different aspects in order to gain knowledge and understanding." Just because your kid is stuck on a single book doesn't mean you can't find ways to make reading more fun for you.

- **MAKE UP SILLY VOICES.** What if the Cat in the Hat sounded like Marlon Brando? Or Elmo had a French accent? Playing around with different voices and sound effects not only gives your inner Meryl Streep a workout, it also helps your child listen to the story in a new way. "The inflections in a mother's voice help children understand the meaning of what she is conveying, so it's not only more interesting but is also easier to follow and understand," Neuman explains. Also, by adding a sense of playfulness to the story, you demonstrate that a book is more than just printed words on a page—it's a tool to inspire creativity and imagination.

- **EDIT AS YOU GO.** You are hereby granted permission to skip a few lines, a paragraph, or entire pages of the book (if you do it

SCHOOL

swiftly, your child will never notice). If it's a longish book, pick a few favorite pages and focus on those, suggests Neuman. "When you're reading to a young child, depth is much more important than breadth," she says. "If he is fascinated with the page about the garbage truck, then just read that!"

- **SPIN-OFF CONVERSATIONS.** To make each telling of the story unique, ask different questions ("What do you think your teddy bear does when you're at school?" "Do you have a favorite kind of truck?"). "The key is to let your child lead the way," says Neuman. "These conversations and comments help children begin to make connections between the stories and their own lives."

Give Kids a Reason to Rhyme

Poetry may give you flashbacks to high school English, but it makes language exciting for kids. "It's imaginative, and kids gravitate toward it," says Tree Swenson, president of the Academy of American Poets. Take some poetic license with your kids—here's how.

- **PICK POEMS KIDS CAN APPRECIATE.** Your child will get the most out of a poem that's right for her age. Dr. Seuss and Shel Silverstein are great for young kids because of their wacky rhymes; try E. E. Cummings or William Carlos Williams for older kids.

- **NOTICE THE SOUNDS.** Kids love rhythm, so show your child if there is a lot of repetition of one letter, or if the poem rhymes.

- **TALK ABOUT THE IDEAS.** Ask, "What are you picturing in your mind?" or "Does anything not makes sense?" to help your child explore the poem's meaning.

- **LEAVE IT OPEN TO INTERPRETATION.** "A poem is not a test or a puzzle," says Swenson. "It means whatever the listener thinks it means." So ask what your child thinks and offer your own ideas!

Real Advice from Real Moms

How Do You Get Your Kids to Do Homework Without Nagging?

"When my son was in elementary school, we made homework a game. We wrote spelling words on paper plates, and when my son spelled them right, we sailed them through the air like Frisbees. Math problems were written on index cards, which were placed on the floor in a pattern. When he got to the last card, it had a small prize attached. It takes more time, but he had straight As five out of six years!"

After-school Activities

You want your daughter to take dance lessons—but does she? Maybe she's cut out to take art lessons instead. How can you sort through all the instruction out there to find out what's right for her, and if she should stick with it? Check out our activity guide.

Ready, Set, Learn!

You and your child have dozens of fun-sounding classes to choose from, but how do you know which activity to choose and when to start? "What's most important is simply exposing kids to a variety of activities so that they'll discover what they like and are good at," says Ellen Booth Church, a Key West, FL-based former teacher and author of *Everything You Always Wanted to Know About Preschool but Didn't Know Whom to Ask*. Want to find the right class for your kid? Here's how.

Dance

? **WHEN IS MY KID READY?** Introduce him to dance concepts, sometimes called "creative movement," at 2 to 3 years old. He can start instruction in ballet, modern, jazz, or even hip-hop at 4 to 5 years old.

? **WHO KNEW?** The running, skipping, and twirling in dance moves can boost reading and math ability because they require counting steps, noting patterns and rhythms, and progressing in a sequence—all skills that are also involved in academics.

? **IS IT FOR MY KID?** If your child spins down the street—rather than preferring to sit quietly in a sandbox—dance may be a good outlet for her physical energy. It's also valuable for kids with language delays because, as Church explains, "They may find it easier to express themselves physically than verbally."

Drama

WHEN IS MY KID READY? She can start with creative dramatics or imagination games at 3 to 4 years old. By age 6, most kids are ready for full-on theater classes.

WHO KNEW? The art of improvising—inventing characters, plots, and dialogue—lays the groundwork for creative writing, storytelling, and independent thinking down the road, Church says. Socially, kids learn to become part of a group, which means cooperating and using some self-control (because not everyone can go first). Kids also get a crash course in listening—they have to pay attention to the lines being said so they can respond accordingly.

IS IT FOR MY KID? Drama is a great outlet for kids who enjoy being the center of attention. "In a class, there are lots of stars, and a child learns that stars shine at different times," says Church. But drama can also be beneficial if your child has trouble expressing emotions—or if the family is going through a divorce, a new baby, or another transition that can leave kids unsettled—because acting can bring those emotions to the surface or help provide a release.

Art

WHEN IS MY KID READY? "Creative arts" (e.g., finger painting) can be introduced between ages 1 and 3, while lessons in technique (e.g., how to work with watercolors) can begin from age 4.

WHO KNEW? Children who take part in an art program improve in a range of literacy and critical-thinking skills,

What Do You Do With All the Art Projects Your Kids Bring Home from School?

"I take pictures of my child with her art projects taped on the wall in the background and then I keep those in a photo album. Some of the better projects I frame and hang up in her room."

"Every day when I return from work, I go through the girls' art. I put one or two pieces that are really special in a folder and toss the rest. Then in June, when school is over, I put the folder in a storage container that I keep in the attic. I now have one folder for each year of my daughters' lives."

according to a recent study from the Solomon R. Guggenheim Museum in New York City. "Art is a precursor to reading and writing because storytelling starts happening," says Church. "They draw a picture and tell an entire story based on these scribbly things. And the scribbles gradually become symbols, letters, words, and full stories"—the building blocks of literacy.

IS IT FOR MY KID? Art, like music, is a universal inclination, but kids who sit still easily for projects and those who tend to graffiti everything in the house may tune in to it more. Painting and drawing can be good for kids who need work on fine motor skills, and art is a great confidence-booster for those with developmental delays.

Music

WHEN IS MY KID READY? Basic music appreciation can start as early as 6 months. You can introduce kids to instrument instruction around age 4.

WHO KNEW? "Music is great for brain development because it not only enhances kids' understanding of language and vocabulary but it also has patterns, rhythms, and sequences that strengthen memory and math skills," says Sally Goldberg, Ph.D., early-childhood education specialist at the Center for Successful Children, a parent-education organization in Scottsdale, AZ. Other research points to music's mellowing qualities—just listening to it can relax an overly active child, says Goldberg.

IS IT FOR MY KID? Music is great for all kids, but may be especially helpful for those with language delays because it engages different parts of the brain than speaking (which is why people who stutter often have no trouble singing), says Church.

SCHOOL

Swimming

WHEN IS MY KID READY? You and your kid can participate in splashing and kicking in a pool or in the ocean at 6 months, and then begin solo or group instruction at age 3.

WHO KNEW? Swimming helps build coordination; it's also a huge confidence-booster, says Goldberg. "Kids understand that it's a valuable life skill, so when they master it, they feel extremely accomplished."

IS IT FOR MY KID? Learning to swim is great exercise for both mind and body, not to mention a basic survival skill, so all kids should give it a shot. The sooner you get kids in the pool, the more comfortable they'll feel getting their head wet, going in the deep end, and eventually swimming (if you wait too long to start, kids can become fearful).

Sports

WHEN IS MY KID READY? Introduce your kid to basic sports moves (e.g. tossing a ball back and forth) around ages 2 to 3, and striking a ball off a tee from 4 to 5. She can play T-ball games from 4 to 7. Hold off on other competitive sports until age 8.

WHO KNEW? Sports actually enhance brain development and functioning, according to Stephen J. Virgilio, Ph.D., author of *Active Start for Healthy Kids*. Exercise primes the brain for learning by increasing circulation and upping the flow of oxygen.

IS IT FOR MY KID? Sports are a great outlet for energetic children, and they can also draw out a child who is socially withdrawn as long as the activity is age-appropriate. "Before age 8, kids are not developmentally ready for competition," Virgilio says, "When something goes wrong—say, they strike out—they see it as a personal failure rather than an athletic failure, and they can't distinguish between the two."

Stick With It or Quit?

Before you throw in the towel on swim class or football, find out *why* your child doesn't like it: Talk with him afterward, when the situation is not so emotionally charged, suggests Goldberg. Maybe the teacher yells or the class is too difficult. "In some cases, you may uncover a problem that's easily fixed," says Goldberg. If your child is preverbal, look at everything from the teacher and students to the timing (is the class close to nap time?). Know your child and gauge his comfort level. "If you can get your child to cooperate, do it," Goldberg says, because your kid will learn and have fun. "But if an activity is causing too much discomfort, stop and try again another time."

How to Raise a Healthy Competitor

School revolves around homework, tests, and school sports—all of which can make kids feel pressured to "be the best." Social psychologist Susan Newman, Ph.D., of Metuchen, NJ, offers advice on how to cheer on your child without creating a must-win monster.

- **GET IN A POSITIVE MIND-SET.** Steer your child away from an adversarial approach by emphasizing that competition is about self-measurement and striving for excellence, rather than showing off or beating out other kids.

- **KNOW YOUR CHILD'S ABILITIES AND LIMITS.** Statements like, "You could have done better than that," or "Why didn't you practice more?" are devastating to kids. Be realistic about your child's abilities so you can help her when she's down, instead of hurting her.

- **DON'T PILE ON THE PRAISE.** A simple "Good job," rather than over-the-top adulation when he gets, say, the highest grade in penmanship, conveys that it's effort that counts. When he doesn't do as well, let him be upset. "Losing is a lesson that prepares kids for life's inevitable ups and downs," says Newman.

- **TELL HER YOU LOVE HER NO MATTER WHAT.** "A big reason kids compete is to impress their parents," says Newman. "They need to hear that a parent's affection doesn't hinge on their success."

SCHOOL

Web Sites and Computer Games

When it comes to your child's intellectual life, the computer isn't necessarily the evil villain that you might think. In fact, it can teach your child some valuable skills. Check out the newest learning strategies below.

---

9 Reasons to Let Your Kids Play Computer Games

For many parents, the mere mention of computer games conjures visions of kids' little brains turning to mush from staring at a screen all day. With studies showing that kids spend more time on the computer than ever before—and that violent games can indeed lead kids to think and act aggressively—parents' worries are understandable. But not *all* computer games are harmful. Although you should mix your child's computer time with other activities, "many positive developments occur when kids play high-quality games," says Marc Prensky, author of *Don't Bother Me Mom—I'm Learning!* Here's an age-by-age look at the various skills children can build from playing these games.

Ages 3 to 5
Electronic games can boost learning by cultivating kids' eagerness to master letters, colors, numbers, shapes, and patterns. What kids learn at this age:

PRE-READING SKILLS Computers are fabulous teachers—able to repeat stories aloud without ever losing patience! Many virtual books feature animation and games, which make reading fun. But skip phonics programs. "They confuse kids who don't yet get that words are made of individual sounds," says James Paul Gee, Ph.D., professor of literacy studies at Arizona State University and author of *What Video Games Have to Teach Us About Learning and Literacy*.

SCHOOL READINESS Preschoolers with access to a computer score 40 percent higher on school-readiness tests, which measure concepts used in school such as time, classification, and direction, says a study at Wayne State University in Athens, OH. Once in the classroom, those same kids do better on cognitive tasks such as grouping objects.

CREATIVITY Drawing on a computer has one major advantage over paint and crayons: The erase button lets kids experiment freely.

Ages 6 to 9

Grade-schoolers can think logically and empathize with others. Games that involve role-playing and missions can help develop their cognitive and social skills. What kids learn:

LOGIC Figuring out how to get a fox over a wall using a rope or a sword may seem silly, but it takes brainpower. "Kids have to form a hypothesis and test it; they have to use the scientific method," says Henry Jenkins, Ph.D., a professor of comparative media studies at the Massachusetts Institute of Technology. And the more kids practice using logic, the better thinkers they become.

SHARPER MEMORY It'll be easier for your child to learn and remember the 112 elements of the periodic table if she's already practiced memorizing the complex details in many computer games.

TEAMWORK AND COMMUNITY "A great feature of recent games is that kids can play cooperatively as partners," says Warren Buckleitner, Ph.D., editor of the *Children's Technology Review* newsletter. Plus, kids are exposed to new ideas—they can tend animals or see where their house is in relation to their country. "Games can inspire kids to think about the broader world, and help them discover other interests," says Kathleen Clarke-Pearson, M.D., a pediatrician in Chapel Hill, NC, and an American Academy of Pediatrics media expert.

Ages 10 to 12

Once kids are old enough to think through what to do in a given situation before acting, the right games will hone their mental and social skills. What kids learn:

MASTERY OF READING "Reading difficulties often occur around fourth grade, when kids encounter more complex language, especially in science," says Gee. Several games require that kids grasp different shades of meaning in complex language. That helps them conceptualize what words mean in new contexts.

RELATIONSHIP TOOLS Some games have characters created to experience emotions as humans do, so kids can learn to process their feelings through them. "One girl I knew would turn her real friends into characters in her *Sims* game, then play-act to explore issues she was having with them," Gee says. "Seeing her friends' points of view gave her a better perspective on her relationships."

HISTORY AND SCIENCE Many programs are based on real facts—so your child can learn about ancient Egypt or baseball while playing, especially if you supplement the games with books on the topic once their interest is piqued.

MySpace Junior

Networking sites such as Facebook are so popular that even your 6-year-old wants his own page. But will he be safe? Disney and Nickelodeon have launched their own child-friendly sites, joining Club Penguin and Webkinz World, where kids can talk to one another (and their favorite characters) in controlled venues. We asked Sharon Miller Cindrich, author of *E-Parenting: Keeping Up with Your Tech-Savvy Kids*, what parents need to know now:

- **THERE *ARE* PROTECTIONS.** Most kid-focused sites have a filter that restricts the exchange of personal info such as phone numbers, addresses, and full names, says Cindrich. On many sites you can even limit what your child can post with a pull-down menu of prewritten phrases, like "I love *High School Musical.*"

- **THE SITES ARE FREE—MOSTLY.** There's generally no cost to join, but you may get hooked into spending dough on upgraded memberships, trading cards, or computer games. "While the sites are free, the companies do use them to advertise to kids," says Cindrich.

- **A WEBKINZ PET NEEDS LOVE TOO.** A virtual creature—like a real pet—can end up becoming your responsibility. When your kid heads off for a sleepover, be prepared to log on so that his creature doesn't lose points or get "sick."

- **KID SITES ARE GOOD TRAINING.** "These sites lay a solid foundation for safety and appropriate use, which will come into play as your kids get older," says Cindrich. "They can open up an ongoing dialogue about what is safe online."

Language

There's no one "right" way to learn language. Did you know, for instance, that you can nurture language development through jokes? Check out the creative strategies for learning language below, and be sure to add a few giggles for good measure.

Look Who's Talking

If you're freaked out by your child's endless solo conversations, relax—in fact, you should encourage this quirky behavior. When 5-year-olds talked to themselves out loud, they were more successful at performing tasks, such as tapping colored pegs in the proper sequence, than when they remained silent, according to a study from George Mason University. Adam Winsler, Ph.D., a professor of applied developmental psychology at GMU, explains that this "private speech" helps hone thinking and problem-solving skills. "Plus, if you listen in, it's a fantastic window into your child's mind," he says.

Is Your Toddler Trying to Tell You Something?

Can your little one blow bubbles or give you a kiss? If so, he's doing more than just being supercute—he's also showing you that he's likely to pick up language quickly, according to a study from Lancaster University in the U.K. "Children who can make mouth movements like sticking their tongue out, using a straw, or blowing bubbles are less likely to have difficulty learning to speak than children who can't perform these tasks," says psychologist Katie Alcock, the study's lead author.

Your youngster also learns to speak by playing make-believe. "When children learn a word, they are learning to associate a sound that can stand for an object (such as 'dog') with an object (such as an animal with a tail that barks)," says Alcock. So playing make-believe helps kids form relationships between words and objects. But don't panic if your child can't perform these tasks yet—in language, as in all else, every kid develops at his own pace.

Learning Languages Early

Does your child's preschool or grade school teach foreign languages? If not, help develop her brain by taking her to playgroups with bilingual kids, or get a bilingual babysitter. "Research shows that kids who studied a second language for two years raised their scores significantly in English and language arts, and slightly in math," says Nancy Rhodes, director of foreign language education at the Center for Applied Linguistics in Washington, D.C. When a child learns a language, even in small doses, the brain activates more pathways to help her grasp new meanings. That sets the stage for more brainpower in *any* subject.

Laugh and Learn

Getting a giggle out of your child can actually help her academically and emotionally, says Louis Franzini, Ph.D., author *Kids Who Laugh: How to Develop Your Child's Sense of Humor.* "Kids who have a good sense of humor are generally more intelligent, more creative, and have higher self-esteem," he says. "Encouraging your child to laugh is as important as encouraging her to eat her vegetables." Kids start developing their sense of humor at just a few months old, when a game of peekaboo is usually enough to elicit lots of smiles. "When your child's a little older, use an item in a way that she knows isn't correct," says Franzini. "Put her socks on your nose, or pretend to make a phone call with a banana." Make up silly rhymes for familiar words, such as

"Daddy-faddy-waddy" and put them into a song. Always encourage your child to tell jokes, no matter how corny they may be—and don't be surprised if she repeats the same joke two or three times. "Kids love repetition," says Franzini. "Just laugh like it's the first time you heard it."

Back to School

How do you get your kids ready for school in the fall? Listen to moms who have developed strategies for getting their children back on the bus—and getting themselves ready, too!

Back-to-school . . . Again!

New friends, new teachers, new routines—making the transition from the lazy days of summer to the school year is chaotic for your kids *and* for you. Get back into the swing of things with fresh ideas from moms who've been there, done that.

Get Your Kids Psyched!

"Two weeks before school begins, I print up small posters with numbers counting down the days, and my kids help me decorate them. On certain days I have events planned—14 days to go is school shopping day, 12 days to go is a special craft project, 10 days to go is an outing to the amusement park, eight days to go is a visit to the library to get a book for the school year, and so on. With all the fun anticipation, the kids get increasingly excited for the big day to finally arrive."

"The week leading up to the first day, I help my kids get in the mood by reading books about going back to school. My favorite is *First Day Jitters*, by Julie Danneberg, which follows a girl as she's getting ready, but we can't see her face.

Real Advice from Real Moms

How Do You Get Your Kids Out of Bed and Ready for School on a Sleepy Morning?

"I keep a spray bottle of lemon water in the fridge—I wake up my four kids by saying, 'Good morning! You have 25 minutes before we have to leave.' If I get no response, I say, 'You have two minutes before the icy water is on your toes!' If there's still no response, I spray their feet with the water bottle. That gets them up and moving."

She's really anxious, wondering what it will be like and if people will like her, and at the end we learn the girl is actually a teacher! It just goes to show that everyone gets a bit nervous about the first day of school."

"I talk with my daughters about how the start of a school year is about new beginnings, new friends, and new opportunities. My oldest will be starting fifth grade this year, so we discussed how it's a great chance for her to let her personality shine through in the new surroundings. I encourage her to approach the new year with a big smile—it's a small thing, but it really does instill her with confidence. When my younger one started at a new school, I told her to walk in like a princess, with grace, confidence, and courage; those words alone were enough to get her excited."

"I talk to my children about all the new things they'll get to do for the first time now that they're entering the next grade. My oldest is starting middle school and will have his first locker, which is a big deal for him, so we're talking about buying a cool lock and other accessories for it."

"My daughter is really social and loves meeting new people, so I make the transition from summer to school easier by reminding her that she'll be seeing all of her old friends and making new ones. We also talk about all the craft projects she'll get to do—we look over old projects hanging on the fridge and on the wall, and we reminisce about when she made them in past classes. Her eyes get really big, and I can tell she's getting excited for the first day."

Get Yourself Ready

"The start of the school year means having to fill out an infinite number of forms—emergency contacts, PTA sign-up, and medical information. And even though all my kids attend pubic school, I have to write checks for school photos, supplies, athletic participation, field trips, and more—it's daunting! To handle it, I commit to spending one morning filling out all of the paperwork. I make the process less painful by treating myself to a nice cup of coffee and something sweet, like a muffin or a scone."

"There's not much preparation necessary because I'm usually excited for back-to-school: For the first time in months I'll have some peace and quiet—no loud, arguing children around! But when I'm feeling weighed down anticipating all the forms I'll have to fill out, plus getting my reluctant kids back into school mode, a little retail therapy always helps. It's mostly for the kids—we go out and buy new clothes and backpacks, and it's fun for me, too!"

"In order to carve the most family time out of each day, I make a conscious effort to be efficient with tasks and chores; I wake up early to make the kids' lunches, I get to work earlier so I can make it home earlier and get dinner prepared at a decent hour. I also run errands during my lunch break so I can head straight home at the end of the day and be with the family. I want my sons to grow up remembering the fun times they had with us throughout their childhood, even if it's just cooking dinner together or lounging around the living room watching movies. Family time is precious."

"Our school hosts a 'First Day,' when the kids get to go see their classroom and meet their new teacher. It's also a good chance for me to meet the teacher, get a feel for him or her, and start a dialogue that will continue through the school year. This face-to-face conversation reassures me that if I have questions or problems, I can feel comfortable approaching the teacher."

"I get anxious about my son beginning a new grade, so I chat with fellow moms so that we can share our angst, vent, and trade tips. As a

Real Advice from Real Moms

How Do You Get Your Kids Out of Bed and Ready for School on a Sleepy Morning?

"My 7-year-old hates to get up in the morning, but I can usually get him out of bed with a reminder of our 'breakfast date.' He loves the one-on-one mommy time, especially since we just welcomed his baby brother into our family."

single widowed mom, I find it helpful to use other parents as sounding boards. We talk about whether or not our kids should take the bus, how much homework they might get, and who we should talk to at school if our kids have problems. Talking these things out makes me realize that every parent has similar concerns about their kids, and when we share them I often realize that many of them are kind of silly, and I'm able to laugh at myself."

Make the First Day Memorable

"I get up early and make a real home-cooked breakfast, and then I pack a special lunch with some little surprise for the kids to find at lunch. And despite increasing protests as they get older, we always snap pictures of them."

"Each year, I make a new page for my son's school scrapbook. I include photos of him on the first day, plus other info such as his height, weight, and shoe size.

Teachers' Top Tips for Starting the Year Off Right

- **KEEP IN TOUCH.** Parent contact is the key to a child's success, so keep the lines of communication open. "Let us know how to reach you," says Natasha Johns, a fourth-grade teacher in Bedford, IN. "Is e-mail best? Should we never call you at work? We need this info so we can be in touch."
- **GET INVOLVED (BUT NOT *TOO* INVOLVED).** It's helpful when you stay up-to-date on classroom notes and events. "Be present by volunteering to help out in the class and by asking us how you might reinforce school lessons at home," says Rice. And to avoid overstepping, she suggests, "stay focused on your own child's development, rather than on that of the other kids."
- **BRING THE LESSONS HOME.** Help your child keep learning when he's at home by creating an environment that reflects the attitude that school is important. "Establish consistent routines—a place to study, a place to keep materials, and a quiet time each evening devoted to schoolwork," says Rice.

SCHOOL

One year, I put in shots of him cutting off his summer 'fro' the night before the first day. It's fun to look back and observe how he's grown and see the various Catholic-school uniforms over the years. As he's gotten older, he's become less tolerant of this ritual, but I remind him that I'm determined to do it until his senior year—I've even threatened to stalk him on campus for his first day of college!"

"For my son's first-day lunch, I cut his sandwich in a funny shape, cover the packaging of the snacks in cool stickers, and include a note from his father and me. In the evening, we all go out to ice cream and share stories from the day. I think it's so important to start off with a positive, excited attitude, because it sets the tone for the rest of the year."

"I have a tradition with my kids that we always go out to a restaurant of their choice for dinner on their first day of school. It's hard to end vacation, start waking up early, and face the homework, so at least the kids get a fun night out on that first day."

Back to School = Back to Stress?

The thought of returning to the grind of homeroom and homework, the anxiety of making friends, and the fear of not liking a teacher can overwhelm almost any kid. And although some back-to-school stressors have been around since we were school-age, others, such as the ever-increasing pressure to score well on statewide exams, are part of today's growing demands on schoolkids.

At the heart of most back-to-school anxiety is the fear of the unknown. After all, in September, almost *everything* is unfamiliar. And since research shows that a heavy load of anxiety can interfere with how well a child learns, it is important to reassure your nervous back-to-schooler. Try these expert-approved ideas on how to do just that.

- **LET SUMMER BE SUMMER.** It can be hard to do this, given how stores start hawking school supplies in July, but waiting until about two weeks before the school bell rings to stock up on notebooks can reduce your child's anxiety. Shopping any earlier prematurely marks the end of summer—and all the fun the season should bring for kids.

- **RECOGNIZE THAT MISBEHAVIOR MAY BE A SIGN OF STRESS.** Like adults, kids don't always know they're stressed; they just feel irritable, says psychologist Tamar Chansky, Ph.D., author of *Freeing Your Child from Anxiety*. In fact, most kids express stress by acting out, which parents often mistake as bad behavior. "If you notice irritability in your child, ask him what's bothering him," says Chansky. Tell him you're there to help him sort out what's on his mind.

- **DON'T WEAR CONCERN ON YOUR FACE.** As parents, we worry when our kids are feeling distraught, but it's critical to appear positive. "You don't want to feed your child's fear that she won't succeed," says Sucheta Connolly, M.D., a child and adolescent psychiatrist at the University of Illinois at Chicago. "Instead, speak matter-of-factly and tell her you're confident she'll be able to manage going back to school even if she's afraid." And be careful how you react to stress in your own life. "If you tend to become distraught when faced with challenging situations, your kids will follow suit," Chansky says.

- **MAKE SCHOOL REAL.** Fears about a new school, classroom, or friends become larger than life in your child's imagination. If at all possible, take her to visit the school to play in the playground and meet her teacher before the first day of classes. If you've recently moved and your child is worried about not knowing any of the other kids, start a playgroup. Fortunately, once school gets under way, most kids get into the swing of things and find that nothing is as awful as they had anticipated.

SCHOOL

CHAPTER SEVEN

Family

Let's be honest: Moms generally rule the family roost. And that's good (think of all the hugs!) and bad (think of doling out all the discipline). Maybe it's time to take a step back and let Dad help—with playtime, dinnertime, and reading time. Siblings can pitch in too; here you'll discover how to help your kids help you! Pets, of course, are also part of the family—but should your 6-year-old get a hamster or a hermit crab? Finally, find out how to have fun as a family, whether at a museum, a concert, a restaurant, or a party.

Dads

Lots of dads get a little skittish around their babies at first, but once they get the hang of hanging with their kids, they're naturals—and an important part of their child's development. Here's important info on the man in your child's life.

Help Fathers Be Dads

Here's the good news: Fathers have almost tripled the hours they spend focused on their kids over the past four decades. And this is great news for you *and* for kids—when they have a close relationship with their father, they're more likely to form intimate relationships as adults, according to a study from the University of Haifa School of Social Work. "Studies have also shown that kids with involved dads are happier, more confident, and more independent," says Armin Brott, author of *Fathering Your School-age Child*. Other studies have shown that kids with active dads even perform better in school and are more likely to attend college. Want to foster more father–child bonding in your family? Check out these rituals and activities that are real-dad-tested—and mom- and kid-approved.

Toddler Time

Horseplay is most dads' forte—a great counterpoint to moms' more nurturing style of interaction—and during the toddler years, those physical skills are in high demand. "Through rough-and-tumble play, kids learn to use their bodies in new ways, which brings new kinds of development and a new spotlight role for the father," says Michael Connor, Ph.D., professor emeritus of psychology at California State University Long Beach. Here's what Dad can do.

Real Advice from Real Moms

What's the Best Gift You've Ever Given for Father's Day?

"I took my daughter to a pottery store and had her make two little handprints on a mug. Then I painted the words 'Hugs for the Best Dad Ever' on it."

"My husband loves things to be clean, so my kids and I washed and shined his SUV. It was a big hit!"

"I gave my husband a photo album in which each page had side-by-side pictures of our boys at each month for the first year of their lives. Rod loved seeing how different the kids looked and comparing how much they grew each month!"

"My girls, ages 2 and 3, love to play a game called 'Chyna Doll' (named after the female wrestler Chyna), in which they wrestle their father to the floor and jump all over him. It's so different from how I play with them. Plus, it teaches the girls trust—they get to roughhouse and be thrown in the air and still know that they're safe."

"Wade is usually the one who gives our 3-year-old daughter, Libby, her bath. That started early on—because he was spending the day outside the house, it was important that there was something simple he could do routinely with the baby. Libby still prefers her dad's brand of splish-splash over mine any day!"

"Since the girls were toddlers, John's been playing a game where he gets down on his hands and knees and acts like a raging bull, head-butting the kids and rolling them around the floor, all while making 'rrr' noises. They pretend to run away but they fall down on purpose because they love to get caught. In another game, he cradles them in his arms and sings 'Rock-a-Bye Baby' while swinging them wildly—really high and fast. I can't even look, but they love it! I think it makes them feel like their dad is nurturing them in a traditional way, but it has a twist that makes it silly and fun."

Preschool Participation

Study after study has shown that the more children are read to, the faster they'll develop vocabulary and listening-comprehension skills. "Even dads that were baby-shy up till now will find it easier to interact with their kids by reading with them," says Brott. Here's what Dad can do.

"When David noticed that our kids, Aaron, 3, and Rachel, 6, could finish sentences—even whole pages—from their favorite books, he started making up silly endings that make them giggle. It's a ritual he does with them every night and that they look forward to. I can hear peals of laughter from down the hall."

"Gregory, my husband, has been the designated book reader to our three kids—now 9, 5, and 2—since the very beginning. Sometimes while he's reading he changes the word 'Mommy' to 'Daddy' because so many of the books feature moms as caretakers, and he wants our kids to see him in that role, too. He does such a good job reading—animating the voices of pirates and giants and generally hamming it up—that there are certain books the kids won't allow anyone but him to read."

School-age Support

Kids are finally at an age where Dad can share some of what *he* loves as well as help kids find their own passions. "When Dad introduces his special interests to kids, he invites them to be part of his world, says Connor. Here's what Dad can do.

"Scott is a private pilot, so it was natural for him to share his love of flying with our daughter, Gabriella, 4. Nearly every weekend they drive up a little hill alongside Los Angeles International Airport. They lie on the grass and watch the planes fly over their heads. Together they shout out a five-second countdown to landing and high-five each other when they see the white smoke from the airplanes' tires as they touch down at high speed."

"My husband has taught our girls to build basic wood structures (small houses), how to prepare dinner (now they all cook together), and how to track animals in nature. Not doing traditionally 'girly' stuff gives my daughters fantastic practical experiences. I see their self-confidence soaring when they say things like 'I know how to use a wood saw, a hammer, and a corner wrench!' or 'I made chicken and pasta for my family last night!'"

"Scott, an illustrator, draws pictures on the paper napkins he packs in my boys' school lunches. For our youngest son, Carter, the illustrations evolved into a cartoon character called Captain Carter. At dinner one night, Carter, then 8, insisted on drawing special napkins for everyone. He wanted to share the love!"

Siblings

Though it can be hard to remember at times, siblings are *good* for each other. You may have to remind your kids of that fact, and follow the advice below on helping keep peace at home.

Put Your Second Child in First Place

Having a child totally rewrites your schedule. Most of your me-time becomes his time. But with number two (and three and four), you're lucky if you get five minutes alone to sing a song together. In fact, in two-child families, younger siblings received 20 to 25 fewer minutes of Mommy and Daddy time each day between the ages of 4 and 13 than the firstborns did, according to a study from Cornell University. Here, tips on how to sneak in some special time with your littler one.

- **BRING HIM ALONG FOR THE RIDE.** For you, it's a trip to the bank, but for your child it's a chance to bend your ear about the new lizard in his class-room. "My husband and I give each of our three kids a turn coming with us to the supermarket," says Teresa Sellinger of Sparta, NJ. "It's special to the kids, and it makes errands less mundane for me."

- **LET YOUR LITTLE ONE STAY UP LATER.** "We assume we should always put the younger child to bed first," says Linda Sonna, Ph.D., a child psy-chologist and author of *The Everything Parent's Guide to Raising Siblings*. "But if she still takes naps during the day, why not put her to bed *after* her older sibling? Even 15 extra minutes of reading together can go a very long way."

- **LISTEN UP.** Make sure younger kids don't get lost in the conversational shuffle. "Often, a parent will ask something, and the older child will answer for the younger one," says Sonna. "Say, 'Gee, I wonder what your little sister thinks of that.'"

● **MAKE THE MOST OF "WAITING" TIME.** "I try to max out the time between picking up my 4-year-old at noon and picking up my 11-year-old at 2:45," says Jennie Fahn of Los Angeles. "We go to the park, play games, or just dance around together."

Put an End to Sibling Battles

You were hoping your children would be buddies—sharing laughs, keeping each other's secrets, sticking up for each other through thick and thin. But they're at it—*again.* They should be natural allies, so why is the playroom a battlefield?

"Siblings are safe people to fight with because kids know instinctively that a family member's love is unconditional," explains Marian Edelman Borden, author of *The Baffled Parent's Guide to Sibling Rivalry.* As distressing as these episodes are to you, they can actually be good for your kids. "To resolve these squabbles, kids need to learn how to express their feelings, negotiate, and find a fair solution—all important skills for getting along with others," says Borden. Here's how to give them those skills (and give yourself some peace).

Power struggles: "He's making me do all his chores!"

THE PROBLEM: Your kid manipulates his younger brother, probably because he's jealous of the attention you give the little guy.

WHY YOU SHOULDN'T LET IT GO: *Both* boys will start to think that it's okay to bully anyone who's smaller or weaker.

WHAT TO DO: First, see if your older child has a legitimate gripe about the amount of chores he has (if so, redistribute the housework). But if he's bossing his little brother around just because he *can,* "remind him that there are privileges to being the oldest—staying up later, getting

How Do You Make Sure Each Child Gets Some "Me and Mommy" Time?

"I've found something that each of my three kids likes to do alone with me. I take my 5-year-old grocery shopping with me, and she feels great because she gets to help. M 3-year-old son loves working outside in the yard with me, so that is our special time, and then I spend time alone with my baby after the other two go to sleep."

"I have four children, so I always take the older ones to their dance and guitar lessons without the siblings. This gives us a good hour on the way there and back to talk in the car. I turn the radio off and ask a lot of questions to keep them talking!"

a bigger allowance—as well as responsibilities, like setting a good example for his little brother," says Peter Sheras, Ph.D., a clinical psychologist and author of *I Can't Believe You Went Through My Stuff.* Then ask him to think of a way to make it up to his brother, such as helping him with homework. You can cut down on jealousy, too, by making sure that you spend time alone with your older child.

Tattle habit: "He had cookies before dinner!"

→ **THE PROBLEM**: Your daughter is always ratting out her brother because it annoys him and makes her look good.

✗ **WHY YOU SHOULDN'T LET IT GO**: Nobody likes a snitch, and if she keeps trying to get others in trouble, it'll be hard for her to make friends.

✓ **WHAT TO DO**: There's no payoff for your daughter if you don't react, so make it clear that unless someone's getting hurt or in danger, you don't want to hear about it. Even if your son did break the rule about eating before meals, disciplining him isn't worth escalating their rivalry. (You can address his behavior with him at a later time, when your daughter isn't around.)

Also, help your son avoid giving her the gratification of getting upset. "Ask him, 'Have you noticed how your sister teases you, and how you react each time? What would happen if you ignored her?'" suggests Michele Borba, Ed.D., a parenting expert and author of *Nobody Likes Me, Everybody Hates Me.*

FAMILY

Stuff sabotage: "He destroyed my Lego fort!"

THE PROBLEM: Your toddler makes a mess of his older brother's things because, like most curious kids, he wants to play with the big kids' stuff.

WHY YOU SHOULDN'T LET IT GO: Kids who don't respect other people's property won't be able to gain anyone's trust.

WHAT TO DO: Having active little kids means accidents happen. So set aside an area that's off-limits to your younger child—a place where his older sibling can put together puzzles or do his homework. Then help your youngest learn the concept of privacy by explaining that some things, such as Mommy's favorite necklace, aren't for sharing.

When he makes a mess of his sibling's things, ask him, "'How do you think your brother feels when you do that?' Then have him draw a happy or mad face to show what he thinks," suggests Myrna B. Shure, Ph.D., a professor of psychology at Drexel University in Philadelphia, and author of *Thinking Parent, Thinking Child*. If your child repeatedly gets into his sibling's things, tell him there will be a consequence, such as a time-out.

Friend feuds: "She won't let me play with them!"

THE PROBLEM: Your younger daughter insists on joining in whenever her older sister has friends over.

WHY YOU SHOULDN'T LET IT GO: She won't get to practice making friends on her own if her sister's pals serve as a ready-made inner circle. Plus, trying to fit in with an older crowd could make her less able to relate to her peers, which is important for her social development.

WHAT TO DO: Help your kids come up with ground rules for when they will play together. For example, when neighborhood kids drop by, everyone hangs out. But if a classmate is coming for a playdate, the other sibling will leave them alone. (Invite a friend for the solo child or plan a project for her.) Another way to manage: When everyone plays in a

"Our girls are 4 and 6, and once a week I take one girl for a 'Mommy date' while my husband takes the other for a 'Daddy date.' We go to the zoo, the park, or the beach, and ice cream is almost always involved. Sometimes they insist that we wear matching outfits and do our hair the same."

"I have five children, from 2 to 10, and each one gets 'lap time.' Even my 10-year-old still wants to climb into the rocking chair with me and tell me about her day. It's only a few minutes of alone time, but it's something they really enjoy."

common space, the more the merrier. But when friends head into the bedroom, they get to be alone.

Physical fights: "Mom, he punched my arm!"

THE PROBLEM: Because it's hard for children to control their emotions, even kids who usually get along can get physical when they're angry.

WHY YOU SHOULDN'T LET IT GO: Kids who are permitted to duke it out learn that might makes right.

WHAT TO DO: Skirmishes often happen when kids are tired or hungry, and ready to melt down. If the predinner hour brings out the beast in them, have them play separately. Whatever the cause, be consistent: You don't allow hurting—ever. (Even play fighting is a no-no since the smaller child often gets hurt.) When a fight erupts, tell them to stay away from each other until they're calm enough not to yell. For preschoolers and older kids, Borba suggests using the "red light, yellow light, green light" method: "They should stop and calm down; use facts, not insults, to explain why they are upset; then discuss what they can do to avoid a fight next time, such as taking turns playing with a toy."

Turf wars: "She's hogging the computer!"

THE PROBLEM: Your kids share a room, and they constantly fight over who gets to use what's in it.

WHY YOU SHOULDN'T LET IT GO: Sharing is the foundation for all the critical social skills kids need, and those who aren't good at it will have a hard time learning compromise, negotiation, and fairness.

FAMILY

✓ **WHAT TO DO:** Toddlers think everything is theirs to play with, so keep your older child's favorite toys on a shelf that the younger one can't reach. Once kids reach preschool age, though, you should help them come up with their own rules for sharing. If, say, they fight over the computer, ask them to think about whether the sister who comes home earlier can go first for a set period, or if they can divide up after-dinner hours into equal chunks of computer time. "Giving kids the tools they need to work out problems makes them feel empowered," says Borba. Not only will they learn to respect others—and you—more, but your kids will also gain a huge sense of pride from settling their differences without always having to get Mom involved.

Advice from an Expert

Siblings are going to fight—as much as 700 percent more with one another than with their friends, because they know their brother or sister will always be there, says journalist Po Bronson, author of *NurtureShock: New Thinking About Children*. It can be torture to watch, he adds, but instead of constantly refereeing or separating kids, a parent's smartest move is to point out activities that siblings can enjoy together. Studies show that kids who play together, even if they're calling each other Poopyface while they do it, go on to have closer relationships than siblings who simply play on their own.

More Love for Your Kids

Caregivers, aunts, uncles, grandparents—they all offer extra love for your child. Here's how to stay in touch and appreciate this extra care.

The Other Woman in Your Child's Life

No matter how much you like and trust your babysitter, day-care worker, or nanny, handing your most precious cargo off to another woman can be a gut-wrenching experience. In her book, *The Perfect Stranger,* Lucy Kaylin, mother of two, explores the complex relationship between moms and caregivers. Her message—to shake your guilt and try to be grateful for your child's sitter or nanny—is easier said than done. Kaylin suggests focusing on the positive aspects of having a caregiver in your child's life: "A day-care worker or nanny is less likely to perceive everything your child does as a reflection on them or as a sign of his future success in life," says Kaylin. "Plus, many child-development experts believe that it's emotionally beneficial for children to be able to form a bond with someone who is not their parent."

Nurture your child's sense of belonging by anchoring her place in your family's heritage. "Telling the history of your names and sharing family stories—especially the funny ones—are good ways to introduce kids to the concept," says Charles Huffine, M.D., a child psychiatrist in Seattle. Other ways to tap into your family's roots: Look through old photos together, or ask an older relative to tell stories to bring family lore alive.

How Do You Help Your Children Bond with Grandparents Who Live Far Away?

"My parents live in India, and we keep photos of them on the refrigerator. That way, when my daughters, ages 6 and 2, speak to them on the phone, they can look right at their faces. It really helps them connect better and understand who they're speaking to."

"I put pictures and videos from school and sports events on our family website so my parents can get a peek at what the boys are doing every day. It helps keep the connection strong until the next face-to-face visit!"

"Ever since my girls were babies, they've spent an entire week with each set of grandparents every summer. At first it was out of necessity—day care was closed—but now we all look forward to it. Now that they're 5 and 7, it's important to us to keep up that wonderful relationship."

Pets

What's better for a child than a pet to care for and love? It all sounds so sweet—but don't forget the realities of who takes care of the pet, how much it costs, and how to comfort your child when his pet dies. Here's what you need to know about all kinds of critters.

Real Advice from Real Moms

How Do You Help Your Child Cope When a Pet Dies?

"When my oldest daughter was 3, we had a baby kitten that passed. We blessed the kitten, put it in a shoebox, and buried it by a maple sapling that we had planted the day before. My daughter is 6 now, and she still talks about that day as if it were yesterday."

"Mommy, I Want a Puppy!"

A boy and his dog—it's an idyllic image of childhood, and for good reason. "Pet relationships can give a child powerful lessons in respect, empathy, and love that last a lifetime," says Rachel Fleissner, M.D., a child and adolescent psychiatrist in Fargo, ND, who offers animal therapy in her practice. Research shows that kids who grow up with animals have more self-esteem, higher IQs, and better emotional health as adults. But you have to choose a pet wisely. What kind of animal should you bring home? Start your search by checking out our family-pet primer.

Fish and Hermit Crabs

GOOD FOR KIDS AGES: INFANT AND UP

Fish and hermit crabs rank low on the cuddly scale, but they still reinforce the link between people and animals. Fish are more interactive than many people think—koi and Oscars can be trained to eat right out of your child's hand! You might want to skip the goldfish, though: They produce so much waste that cleaning the tank can become a real chore. Guppies and tetras are better starter fish. With hermit crabs, kids 5 and up get a great intro to science when the crabs change shells, which they do as often as every two days.

PROS: Fish are naturally soothing. They're also low maintenance, thus great for busy families.

CONS: A fish or crab doesn't offer the same emotional and physical comfort as a furry pet, so your child is less likely to treat it as a confidant.

CARE REQUIRED: Hermit crabs, like fish, thrive in groups. So get a few (you'll need a two-to-five-gallon tank). Tanks for both pets need cleaning weekly. Your total annual expenditure: $200 to $350 for food and maintenance.

WHAT YOUR CHILD CAN DO: Toddlers can help with feeding and older kids can clean out the tanks with supervision.

Guinea Pigs, Hamsters, Gerbils, and Rabbits

GOOD FOR KIDS AGES: 8 AND UP

Because they're so small and soft, it's easy for these mammals to be mishandled and even hurt, so they're not ideal for young kids. These animals thrive on being held, touched, and spoken to, so kids can enjoy an affectionate relationship with them.

PROS: Since each type has different traits—hamsters, for instance, are nocturnal—kids learn to appreciate and respect differences in others.

CONS: Most of these little furballs only live for five years or so. They require a special diet and cage setup (see "Care required," below). And gerbils and hamsters can cannibalize each other if their cages become overcrowded or male dominated, which can be a traumatic scene for young kids.

CARE REQUIRED: These active animals need room in their cages to run around. They also need fresh vegetables for snacks, as well as supplements. Rabbits should be spayed and litter box–trained, and your house has to be rabbit-proofed. Your total annual expenditure: $200 to $250 a year for food, toys, and bedding.

Real Advice from Real Moms

How Do You Help Your Child Cope When a Pet Dies?

"When my daughters' 2-year-old purple betta fish died, both my kids drew a big, colorful picture of him and then wrote a letter saying how much they loved and missed him. They also told him all about the new blue betta fish they were going to get next."

"When our dog had to be put to sleep, it hit my 3-year-old very hard. I read her a poem called 'The Bridge,' about how when a pet dies, it goes to a place just outside of heaven, where it becomes young and healthy and waits for you to come pick it up before you can both go across the bridge to heaven together. It gave her something to think about in a positive way."

"When my daughter's hamster, Chi, developed a tumor, I brought her with me to the vet to have him put down. She held him, kissed him good-bye, and we all cried. Then we brought him home and buried him in the backyard, where she could visit him whenever she wanted. I told her that the hurt will never go away, but it will get better in time, and that Chi is always in our hearts and minds."

✔ **WHAT YOUR CHILD CAN DO:** With supervision, kids can clean cages and feed these animals; with practice, 9- or 10-year-olds can handle them alone.

Birds

GOOD FOR KIDS AGES: 8 AND UP

Because they can be unpredictable and quick to nip, birds are not good pets for young kids. Children adore the smaller varieties, like parakeets and cockatiels, because of their clever mimicking skills. But your family had better love birds, because large ones can live 50 years or more, and small birds live 15 to 20 years. And since birds travel in flocks, you need at least two so they have company.

➕ **PROS:** Birds are highly intelligent and easily tamed and trained. But best of all, they're beautiful and funny. And you can't beat the fascination factor when kids see the birds fly.

➖ **CONS:** Birds are a lot of work. Even with daily cleaning, cages can be an eyesore when birds muss their bedding.

♥ **CARE REQUIRED:** Buy the largest cage you can. Birds should be let out to fly around the house at least once a day. (Watch out for droppings!) They also need a fortified pellet mix rather than seeds (which are unhealthy as a bird's sole diet), fruit, and veggies. Your total annual expenditure: $750 for food, toys, and supplements.

✔ **WHAT YOUR CHILD CAN DO:** Birds love chitchat, so your child should talk to them daily. Older kids can handle a tamed bird with supervision, and kids of any age can help clean the cage.

Cats and Dogs

GOOD FOR KIDS AGES: 5 AND UP

Dogs and cats offer complete, unconditional love. Wait until your child is 5 before you get a cat or a dog, though; before that, kids don't

FAMILY

Kids love the idea of these unusual pets, but veterinarians warn that they can be a hazard to the entire family.

- **TURTLES, IGUANAS, AND OTHER REPTILES.** Reptiles can secrete salmonella bacteria, putting all but the most meticulous hand washer at risk.

- **POT-BELLIED PIGS.** Years ago, these intelligent swine were media darlings, squired around by celebrities such as George Clooney. But many grow to 200 pounds or more and can become very aggressive toward children and anyone else they outsize.

- **MACAWS, PARROTS, AND OTHER LARGE BIRDS.** These birds tend to bond with one person, so they're not great for families. And when they get angry, their bites are powerful enough to take off an ear or finger.

understand that animals have feelings, and your child may inadvertently hit or hurt the animal. It's also crucial that you find a animal with a temperament that meshes with your entire family. Generally, smaller breeds aren't as fond of kids as larger dogs are. An animal that's at least 8 months old is often a better choice than a pup or kitten because its personality is established, so you know what you're getting. And be sure to research each breed's habits. You'll quickly discover which dogs bark the most and which cats are noisiest at night.

PROS: Dogs and cats are loyal friends, so they can teach kids devotion and steadfastness.

CONS: These pets require lots of attention. So if your family tends to be out of the house a lot, they're not for you.

CARE REQUIRED: Cats and dogs need daily exercise (15 minutes of play-time for cats and at least one walk a day for dogs), and regular vet visits. Your total annual expenditure: $800 to $1,500, depending on the size of the animal, for food, medical care, toys, and gear.

WHAT YOUR CHILD CAN DO: A 5- to 8-year-old can help with feeding, and brush the animal, with supervision. By 12, most kids can handle all the care.

Fun as a Family

Why leave your child at home when you can easily take him out on adventures with you? Just be sure to follow the helpful guidelines below, where you'll also find great ways to bond as a family.

Kids: Don't Leave Home Without Them

You may be wary of taking your kids along on adult outings, but these trips can be rewarding for every member of the family, and offer important benefits for your child: Going to grown-up events makes children feel special, exposes them to new experiences, and teaches them how to cope and thrive in unfamiliar situations.

First piece of advice: Relax. If you're stressed, your child is likely to pick up on that and be stressed, too. And a little preparation never hurts. Here's tried-and-true advice from insider experts and real moms on how to take kids anywhere.

A recipe for dining-out success.
Just because your child favors mac and cheese doesn't mean he can't develop an appetite for slightly finer dining.

 **HOW TO PULL IT OFF:** Places with a fairly high noise level, as opposed to quiet, white-tablecloth joints, are good bets—they're casual and kids love the energy, and you'll love that the noise masks any outbursts. Go in the early evening before the crowds arrive, suggests Sara Andrews, a nursery-school teacher who moonlights as a waitress at an upscale eatery in Brooklyn. And bring toys to help keep your child occupied. Cathy White of El Dorado, CA, takes a "restaurant survival pack": a pencil box

with some nonmessy art supplies and fun stickers that are reserved just for restaurants. Another key to an enjoyable experience: interaction. Point out interesting things in the restaurant and discuss with your child which foods you're going to eat. If your child feels ignored, whining or a tantrum is practically guaranteed.

Ⓧ BIGGEST SABOTEURS: "Dining out is a sedentary experience, so it can be a challenge for a toddler who wants to practice his exciting new motor skills," says Stefanie Powers, a child-development specialist at Zero to Three, a nonprofit children's research center in Washington, D.C. Request a table near open space so your child can walk around. And order an appetizer that can be prepared quickly so he doesn't have to wait too long for food. Many restaurants will whip up a child-friendly dish—buttered pasta, a mini burger—even if it's not on the menu.

Shopping-spree smarts.

Shopping teaches kids crucial real-life skills: interacting with others (such as the sales staff) and paying for things you buy, says Powers.

✓ HOW TO PULL IT OFF: Go when your child is fully rested—after a nap or in the morning. Before you go, map out kid-friendly lunch spots where you can take a break, or bring a (nonmessy!) snack from home and rest on a bench. And get your child involved: Darlene Link, a clinical psychologist in King of Prussia, PA, allows her daughter to try on clothing, and teaches her what "on sale" and "cheap" mean.

Ⓧ BIGGEST SABOTEURS: Even a mall filled with stuff can get tiresome to a kid. To buy more shopping time, promise a small reward. Say, "Once Mommy finds the skirt, we'll look for a Hello Kitty store." Says Link, "It's a lesson in patience and how things work. 'I help Mommy with this now, she'll help me do what I want later.'"

Sweet music to little ears.

At concerts, "Children will hear sounds they want to make themselves, and see instruments they are interested in," says Bonnie Simon, co-creator of the children's symphonic music series *Stories in Music,* from Magic Maestro Music. "And if it's a great concert, a child will be touched to the very depth of his soul."

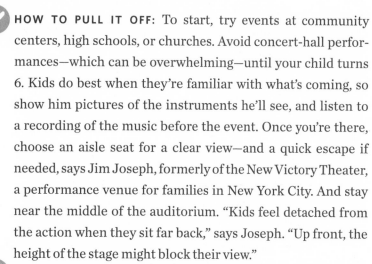 **HOW TO PULL IT OFF:** To start, try events at community centers, high schools, or churches. Avoid concert-hall performances—which can be overwhelming—until your child turns 6. Kids do best when they're familiar with what's coming, so show him pictures of the instruments he'll see, and listen to a recording of the music before the event. Once you're there, choose an aisle seat for a clear view—and a quick escape if needed, says Jim Joseph, formerly of the New Victory Theater, a performance venue for families in New York City. And stay near the middle of the auditorium. "Kids feel detached from the action when they sit far back," says Joseph. "Up front, the height of the stage might block their view."

BIGGEST SABOTEURS: Little kids often get scared of the darkness when the lights dim in the concert hall, says Joseph. Arrive early to allow your child to grow accustomed to the space, and explain what's happening when the lights go down.

Let's party!

Who doesn't enjoy a festive evening? Jenny Coniff of Clinton, CT, says her 5-year-old son "loves feeling that he's part of a fun 'big boy' event" at adult parties. Link likes watching her shy daughter open up at such events. "Once she's comfortable, she loves it," says Link.

HOW TO PULL IT OFF: Ask your host if it's okay to bring your child. And don't assume that a yes means kiddie activities and food will be provided, says Debi Lilly, owner of Chicago's A Perfect Event, an event-planning service. Buy inexpensive toys, candies, and fun snacks just for the party, and bring your child's favorite movie in case she needs some quiet time. Once there, greet the host and familiar faces together so your child feels more comfortable, but don't say hello to everyone—it'll likely overwhelm her.

⊗ BIGGEST SABOTEURS: Trintje Gnazzo, a Winchester, MA, mother of two, has observed that the more fun the party is for adults—say, a cocktail shindig—the more attention-getting behavior and tantrums kids exhibit. So take notice of your child's needs, and take time out to play together or let her run around outside.

Teach Your Child to Love Art

A trip to an art museum is a great way to spend a chilly winter day—even for toddlers. Follow these tips from Susan McCullough, director of School and Family Programs at New York City's Museum of Modern Art.

- **GIVE A PREVIEW.** Log on to the museum's Web site and ask your child to pick out the pieces she wants to find. "Kids love to be able to go to the museum and see works they've seen somewhere else," says McCullough.
- **STREAMLINE YOUR VISIT.** Once you're at the museum, look for a family guide to help you find other kid-friendly works. Just keep your visit to about an hour so your child doesn't get burned out.
- **LET HER PLAY THE ARTIST.** "Stand in front of a Jackson Pollock painting and ask your kid to trace the lines in the air," says McCullough. "That gets her to look more closely at the work." Another way to engage your child: Bring a sketchbook and pencil, and have her draw pictures of what she sees."
- **STRETCH HER IMAGINATION.** Help her connect with a work by asking her to make up a story about it. If she's looking at a landscape painting, ask, "If you were writing a postcard from here, what would you say?" Getting those creative juices flowing is what art is all about—for you and your child.

"On days when the weather doesn't cooperate, I do yoga with my daughter in our basement. She chooses the poses, which are always animal-related. Our favorites are the Camel pose, the Dead Bug pose, and the Butterfly pose. She is infinitely more flexible than I am, but she has less patience, so we are a balanced team. The only problem we run into is when our dogs try to join in—our session ends up erupting into silliness instead of calm!"

• **WATCH OUT FOR FATIGUE.** Mike Norris, an educator at New York City's Metropolitan Museum of Art, cautions that fatigue can be easy to miss since you may not notice how much distance you're covering. Depending on your child's age, plan to leave after 30 minutes to an hour.

14 Fun—and Memorable— Ways to Bond as a Family

When things are so hectic that you barely get the kids to school on time and keep the fridge stocked, it's hard to squeeze in regular family rituals. But creating and maintaining traditions, big and small, can help bring families closer. Rituals that celebrate holidays and milestones can also help reinforce your family's passions and beliefs, giving your kids a sense of belonging to something bigger than themselves. Traditions don't need to be elaborate or expensive to be meaningful. Check out these ideas from moms around the country for inspiration.

Everyday Ways to Stay Close

"HOW WAS YOUR DAY" DINNER "Every night, we go around the dinner table and ask each of our five children to tell something interesting or exciting that happened that day. The exchange often lasts into the third round of cookies for dessert, but no one leaves the table until everyone has had a turn. The kids know they get to share a portion of their day with the family, and my husband and I learn things we might not otherwise know about."

CONVERSATION BASKET "We have a conversation basket we use a few times a week at dinner to encourage lively discussions. I started it by writing ideas on pieces of paper, like 'Name one thing you learned today.' Now we all contribute questions. It makes dinnertime an adventure—we don't know what the question will be or how each person will respond—and it sparks our creativity, because you have to really think before answering."

BEDTIME KISSES "Every night, I give my children three 'magic' kisses before bedtime and say, 'I like you,' 'I love you,' and 'I'll always protect you.' I've done this since they were born. Even on those nights when I have to yell 30 times for them to get to bed, and I may be angry, they know with the kisses that I still love them. It helps them feel safe and secure."

Weekly and Monthly Rituals

PAJAMA WALKS "We live in the country, and every Sunday morning, we walk the fields on our property wearing our flannel pajamas. We talk about everything, from what's happening at school to which wildflowers are in bloom. It's sacred, uninterrupted time to appreciate all we've worked for—and each other."

INDOOR CAMPING "Our family tradition is camping . . . in the living room on the weekends! We turn out the lights and use flashlights, and have popcorn and a movie. Then we snuggle in and talk about the week. My son talks about it regularly during his kindergarten's show-and-tell."

FAMILY FUN NIGHT "Every weekend, we have family fun night—one family member gets to choose the evening's activity. The boys often choose sports-related outings, such as hockey games at our local university or ice-skating. They love planning an event for the family. No matter what the person in charge that week comes up with, everyone participates, even if they're not crazy about the idea. The experiences keep our family ties strong and become part of our shared family history."

BLENDED-FAMILY BONDING "On Friday nights, my husband goes downstairs with his two kids to play games or watch a movie, and I do

Real Advice from Real Moms

How Do You Bond as a Family?

"I take my kids on a treasure hunt after dinner. On a piece of paper, I write numbers from 1 to 4. Next to each number I'll write an object and draw a simple picture of it. For example: 1 stone, 2 acorns, 3 leaves, 4 twigs. I then give each of my children a bag and we go around the neighborhood and try to collect all the items in the quantities stated. Being in nature with my kids soothes me and gets us all on the same page."

the same upstairs with my children. We do this to honor and recognize our 'old' families—the families we were before we came together. This actually helps keep our stepfamily close by showing that we appreciate all of the family configurations that we had previously and have now. The kids appreciate that we haven't forgotten the old ties."

FAMILY MVP "We have a 'Cunningham of the Month' award, and we all vote on each month's winner. I make a poster with the person's photo surrounded by funny comments about that month's winning deed, then display it on the refrigerator. The first award went to my oldest son for using a fishing pole to reel in his brother's remote control boat from the middle of a small pond. All month long, the anticipation builds as we talk about who should get the award and why. It makes everyone feel special, and the kids love the recognition."

MOTHER-SON DATES "On Thursday afternoons, I pick up my son early so he can spend time alone with me, apart from his sister. We call it 'going on a date.' There's no set agenda—we'll get juice, then we might go for a walk or do errands. Sometimes he'll open up and talk to me; sometimes not. It's important to him that we have time together when there's no one else competing for my attention, because that's how it used to be before Sophia was born. As we drive away from his school, I can sense him relaxing, knowing that it's our special time."

Annual Traditions

BIRTHDAY-DINNER TOASTS "At dinner, we toast the birthday girl, and everyone gathered at the table says a few words of appreciation. I also create a table centerpiece that represents the birthday girl's life, including photos from throughout the year and various items reflecting her interests. My daughters roll their eyes a bit now that they're getting older, but I know our family's birthdays wouldn't be the same without this ritual."

FAMILY

SUMMER ROAD TRIP "My daughter and her best friend go to sleep-away camp every summer. Before they leave, both moms and daughters take a trip to an Orlando theme park. We're together for a few days and have countless conversations about issues like peer relationships and politics. As a parent and psychologist, I value these moments as a way to connect. It's a tradition we look forward to every year."

MEMORABLE ADVENTURES "Every year before school starts, our family goes on a surprise adventure day to someplace within a two-hour drive of our home. It's a fun way to spend time together before we get caught up in school activities, and a great way to create shared memories. We always take lots of pictures. Then, a few months later, the kids and I create pages for their scrapbooks using the photos and other souvenirs. We spend time together both on our adventure day and then later when we relive our memories as we work on our scrapbooks."

BACK-TO-SCHOOL FAMILY DINNER "The night before the first day of school, I prepare a fancy dinner. We use our good china, candles, and table linens, and the whole family is required to wear their dress clothes. During dinner, we talk about the year ahead, kicking off the school year in a fun, comforting way that makes it special. Plus, it helps keep the lines of communication open all year long by showing our kids we're interested in making the school year a positive experience."

HARVEST MOON CELEBRATION "On the night of the harvest moon each fall, my sons and I play together in the moonlight. This originally came about many years ago because my younger son was afraid the moon was falling from the sky. It's a ritual that's uniquely ours: We've made up games like 'harvest moon ball' (a cross between baseball and tag) and have gone to the playground or had picnics in the backyard. We look forward to planning our harvest moon ritual each year—it's special mother-son time."

Real Advice from Real Moms

Helping Kids Help You

Encouraging your children to do tasks around the house each evening not only takes the edge off those stressful hours, it also increases kids' self-esteem and independence, explains Elizabeth Bailey, a family therapist in New York City. Here, some of the ways real parents get their kids to share the load.

"When my 6-year-old daughter was a toddler, I always let her 'help' with the bath routine. I'd take her clothes off, and she'd put them in the laundry hamper. Then I'd take the diaper off, tape it up, and she'd carry it to the diaper pail and drop it in. To this day, I never have to ask her to put her dirty clothes away."

Help Around the House

No, you *don't* have to do it all, at least not around the house. Check out these tips for making your evening—and your whole house—run more smoothly with a little help from experts *and* your family.

5 Steps to Calmer Evenings

Whether you work outside the house or stay at home full-time, the toughest part of the day is the same: those frantic early evening hours when there are mouths to feed, homework to do, and cranky kids to handle. The trick is to streamline your to-do's so you can feel calmer and focus on what counts—spending time with your family. Here's how.

1. **EASE INTO THE EVENING.** Instead of walking in the door after work or errands and immediately launching into another chore, allow time and space to downshift into evening mode. "What we are dealing with here is the need for transition," explains Julie Morgenstern, author of *Time Management from the Inside Out*. "Giving yourself and your family that unwind time can completely change the feel of the evening." Creating a calming ambience—by, say, turning off the TV and playing soothing classical, jazz, or instrumental music—can instantly reset the emotional tone of the house. A fun ritual—like a "cocktail hour" with a plate of veggies and dip and wine or water in fancy glasses—can also ease everyone into family time.

2. **CREATE A DINNER SYSTEM.** Rushing to get dinner on the table—and the last-minute "What am I making?!" freak-out that goes with it—is a major source of evening mayhem, but a little bit of preplanning can help you power through with a minimum of stress. Morgenstern recommends using the weekends to chart out your nightly dinners, grocery shop, and even preassemble parts of a meal when possible. Consider writing a weekly plan and checking the calendar to see which nights are going to be particularly busy—so you know when frozen pizza or easy-prep meals are a must. Next, post the week's schedule on the refrigerator, where you can easily see what's on the horizon long before the dinner hour hits.

3. **KEEP THE KIDS BUSY.** You may need a little creativity to get the kids out from underfoot. One mom encourages her family to take their pre-dinner "cocktails" into the family room for some quiet time. With children younger than 5, you might find it easier to involve them in what you're doing.

4. **PLAN HOMEWORK TIME.** To avoid last-minute cries of "Mom, I haven't done my homework yet," institute some planning in the academic department as well. Morgenstern recommends providing a comforting, reliable workspace for your children—and a set hour in which to do homework. "If your kids like to study on the living room floor, clear out a cabinet in the entertainment center for pens, paper, and books, and keep it well-stocked, she says. When setting your kids' homework time, be sure to take into account your *own* tolerance for multitasking. If your kids are younger and need more help with their homework, having them do it while you cook dinner means you'll be constantly running back and forth. "Anticipate their need for attention and spend homework time doing a task that you can easily break away from, like reading a magazine or folding laundry," says Morgenstern.

Real Advice from Real Moms

Helping Kids Help You

"When I empty the dishwasher each night, I have my 18-month-old daughter take the plates out from the bottom rack. She also enjoys taking the clothes out of the front-loading washer and putting them in the dryer. This makes her feel like she's got my undivided attention, yet we're both doing 'chores.'"

"I established a ten-minute, before-bed cleanup routine for my 6- and 2-year-olds. We put on music to make it fun, and I assign tasks, like 'put those blocks in that box,' to each of them while we dance around. It's really helped my sanity, and gets the house clutter-free for the next day."

5. **SHARE THE WORK . . . AND A BREAK.** Dividing tasks between you and your husband can make family time more serene for both of you. Your guy might not exactly be volunteering for more evening duties, but asking him to do something within his comfort zone can help. If your husband is stressed when he first walks in the house (and you're not), offer him a later-in-the-evening task, such as washing dishes while you're putting the kids to bed. If he doesn't mind helping with homework but is useless in the cooking department, consider making dinner while *he* hits the tutoring table. And remember, too, that it's okay to switch off; what works initially may grow tiresome after months of daily repetition.

Good Clean Fun

Whether you're entertaining or just doing your routine cleaning, you don't have to chase every last dust bunny yourself. Here, advice on getting kids to roll up their sleeves and pitch in from Tara Aronson, author of *Mrs. Clean Jeans' Housekeeping with Kids.*

- **DO A FEW TRIAL RUNS.** If you're hosting a party, don't wait until the last minute to clean. Get your child used to the routine a few days before the event.

- **GIVE THEM A CHOICE.** Your child will be more motivated to help if she gets to choose her tasks. Make a list of chores and let each family member pick what they want to do—or dread doing the least!

- **SHOW SOME RECOGNITION.** Create a chart of chores, with pictures for each task (such as the messy dining table that needs to be set). When your child performs a task, he can put a sticker over the picture. Reward him with an activity of his choice when he's completed all chores.

- **MAKE A GAME OUT OF IT.** The more fun kids have, the more they'll help. So invent different cleaning games. For instance, he can play "Onesie," where he has to pick up every object of one type, such as anything that's blue—it's not as helpful as dusting the living room, but every little bit counts!

CHAPTER EIGHT

Holidays

T he twinkling lights! The delicious smells coming from the kitchen! The never-ending work and the inevitable meltdowns! Yes, the holidays are here. Thankfully, this chapter shows you and your kids how to handle the stress that goes hand in hand with this time of year. You'll also find great advice on teaching kids the joy of giving and drawing on their strengths to create age-appropriate ways to give. And what holiday is complete without family traditions and picture-perfect holiday cards? Here's all you need to know to make your holidays merry and bright!

Stress

Remember when you were a kid and holidays were nothing but fun? No matter how stressed you get during the so-called festive season, it's important to keep the tension level low for your kids, so they can truly love this special time. These tips will help you and your kids dial down the stress.

Take the Stress Out of Santa Season

Children can get just as frazzled as their parents during the holidays, leading to insomnia, tummy aches, and temper tantrums. Here, eight easy expert-recommended ways to ensure a happy, healthy holiday for the entire family.

1. **SEND YOUR OWN STRESS PACKING.** Kids take their emotional cues from adults, and no matter how hard we try to hide our own stress, they can pick up on the tiniest of signals—a quick sigh or tight facial expression. Plus, because younger children are inherently self-centered (a normal developmental stage), they tend to blame themselves for our angst, which only stresses them out more. Don't ignore your own mental health, advises Carol Kauffman, Ph.D., an assistant clinical professor at Harvard Medical School. "Check in with yourself to make sure your expectations for the holidays aren't too high," she says. For instance, rather than running yourself ragged trying to find the perfect gift for a girlfriend, settle on a gift card at a store you know she'll love, and remind yourself that she'd never want you to put yourself through the wringer. And if you're feeling that overwhelming urge to stomp on the tangled Christmas lights and cancel the holidays altogether, just stop, and treat your child to a back or foot rub. Massage stimulates pressure receptors under the skin in *both* of you, which slows heart rate and lowers production of the stress hormone cortisol, according to studies at the Touch Research Institute at the University of Miami School of Medicine.

How Do Your Kids Help Out with Thanksgiving Dinner?

"I assign each of my kids a different task: My 10-year-old daughter is in charge of table design, my 12-year-old son is in charge of food placement on the buffet, and my 3-year-old son is in charge of the extras, like filling the gravy boat and helping me make delicious deviled eggs."

"My daughter helps mash potatoes, set the table, and pour the drinks into special glasses she has picked for everyone. She also loves to figure out a new way to fold our napkins each year."

2. **DOLE OUT HOLIDAY TO-DO'S.** "A big source of kids' holiday anxiety comes from feeling like they're lost in the shuffle," notes Jana N. Martin, Ph.D., a child and family psychologist based in Long Beach, CA. But giving each of your children a few special season-centric roles fills them with a calming sense of purpose and belonging. Assign tasks that suit their personalities—for instance, a crafty son may enjoy making a decoration for the front hall—then make each task an annual ritual. "Doing these traditions year after year helps kids develop a sense of mastery, which is in itself comforting," says Martin.

3. **DON'T LET HUNGER HAPPEN.** The holiday ham may be scheduled to hit the table at 7 p.m., but if your child's normal mealtime is 6 p.m., feed him then. "Giving your kids meals and snacks at regular intervals keeps blood sugar regulated and nerves on an even keel," explains Shawn Talbott, Ph.D., author of *The Cortisol Connection Diet.* If he's edgy and mealtime is still an hour or two away, tide him over with a dairy snack such as yogurt or a grilled cheese sandwich. "Although the exact mechanism is unclear, studies show that certain proteins in dairy products have a calming, sedative effect," says Talbott.

4. **KEEP THEM POSTED ON BIG PLANS.** Change is unsettling no matter your age: Would *you* want to trade your bed for a cot so Uncle Ira can be comfortable? Nope, and neither does your little one. So when her life is about to be disrupted, give her a heads-up, but without making too big a deal about it. That in itself can whip up worry by making her think something must be wrong, says Martin. "Instead, start by providing a truthful reason for the change that makes sense to your children," she suggests. For example, explain that Uncle Ira has a bad back and needs a soft mattress. Then point out what *won't* change. ("We'll put your favorite sheets on the cot, and you can still play in your room during the day.")

5. **FALL BACK ON ROUTINE.** "Kids crave structure because it's soothing when they can predict what's going to happen next,"

notes Martin. But impromptu gatherings and unexpected house-guests make sticking to every routine nearly impossible. "Instead, aim to keep at least some aspect of the routines your child is accustomed to," says Martin. For instance, if you can't tuck them in at their regular time, keep up at least one typical pre-bed ritual, like a bedtime story or a glass of warm milk. "This lends focus to the chaos," says Martin. "Kids know that no matter what else is going on, this is something they can count on."

6. **GIVE THEM FREEDOM TO FROLIC.** "Over-scheduling activities can lead to tense and anxious kids," notes Ruth Peters, Ph.D., a child and adolescent psychologist based in Clearwater, FL. And since stress over a prolonged period taxes the immune system, it may even result in physical ailments, such as colds or flu. "Set aside two hours each day for kids to be kids, and avoid scheduling back-to-back or even daily holiday activities," suggests Peters. Also, consider getting a babysitter for at least some of the adult events you know they won't enjoy—for example, the kind where they have to dress up or keep quiet for too long.

7. **LET THE WINTER GAMES BEGIN.** Experts estimate that kids burn about half as many calories in winter as they do in warmer months, due in large part to a drop in physical activity. But exercise is proven to help relieve stress: It unknots tense muscles and triggers the release of endorphins, mood-boosting brain chemicals. So bundle them up and send them outside for an afternoon of building snow forts or sledding, or set up a game of at-home bowling with empty plastic water bottles and a foam rubber ball.

8. **GIVE HER AN ESCAPE PLAN.** If your child is particularly shy in big groups or around new people, agree on a secret code word or gesture she can use to quietly send you an SOS, such as tapping your thumb or taking your hand, suggests Martin. This way, she can tell you that she needs you without calling attention to herself and causing embarrassment. The best part: Just knowing that this option is available to her will put her at ease.

Real Advice from Real Moms

How Do Your Kids Help Out with Thanksgiving Dinner?

"We put heavy whipping cream in a big Mason jar and all the kids take turns shaking it until it turns to butter. This keeps them busy and they love doing it every year—even now that all four are teenagers!"

"I let them play video games to keep them out of my way. That goes for my husband too!"

Gifts

Grab your child's hand and take a giant leap beyond ordinary giving this holiday season: show them how to give back. It will help your child understand the value of giving, and stop the gimmes dead in their tracks. Here's how.

Teach Your Kids the Gift of Giving

Of course kids love getting presents at the holidays, but what truly makes the season special is the genuine sense of goodwill all around them. That's why the holiday season is the best time to show a child how to spread that warmth by helping others. Yes, it's great for the needy, but it's even better for your kid. Children love being helpful (it makes them feel grown-up), and volunteering "gives them the chance to experience the deeply rewarding payoff that comes from making someone else happy," says Deborah Spaide, author of *Teaching Your Kids to Care*. When your child gives, he gets . . .

- **COURAGE TO INITIATE CHANGE.** When a child improves someone else's life, he sees that he can change the world around him—and even himself—for the better, says Cathryn Berger Kaye, author of *The Complete Guide to Service Learning*. For 6-year-old Cleo of Pelham, NY, volunteering at her local park has shown her the big impact of a small gesture. "A park is nice and relaxing, but if it's all messed up, no one wants to come there," she says. "I like burying the bulbs so there can be flowers again."

- **COMPASSION FOR ALL BEINGS.** Helping people in need lets kids flex their caring instincts. Same goes for working with animals. "The kindness, understanding, and patience that kids learn in caring for pets segues to gentleness with peers," says Charlotte LeFrank, program coordinator at the Child Abuse Prevention Council in Windsor, Ontario. Danny, 12, of North Andover, MA, spread the kindness message at his "ASPCA birthday party" by asking friends to bring toys for the animals at a local shelter rather than gifts for him. "The animals were so bored, and I have a whole room of things to play with," says Danny, who has two cats adopted from his local ASPCA.

- **ENTHUSIASM FOR TEAMWORK.** Working with others toward a common goal shows kids that sharing responsibility can have a bigger impact than going it alone. Take 7-year-old Natalie of Seattle. To aid tsunami victims, she spearheaded a fundraising bake sale at her school. "I like working with my friends, and it was easier with people helping," she says. "It made me feel really good to help people I didn't know."

- **POWERFUL PRIDE.** Volunteering is a win-win experience for kids: Every little bit they do helps, and that, in turn, is a great self-esteem booster. "Realizing they did something to make someone else smile is priceless," says Spaide. "You can't match that feeling."

How to Plant the "Giving" Seed

It's never too early to expose your child to philanthropic activities, says Kathy Saulitis, senior director of youth and family at Kids Care Clubs, a group that promotes volunteering. To motivate them to give back, follow these expert tips.

Real Advice from Real Moms

How Do You Keep Your Child from Getting Caught up in the "Gimmes"?

"We take the focus off gifts by discussing the historical story of Hanukkah with our girls, and we also plan a lot of activities that don't involves 'gimmes,' like making latkes and homemade applesauce, making a menorah out of clay, and spinning the dreidel."

"Our family has a tradition of opening up one present at a time, and then hugging the person who gave it and telling them 'thank you' before moving on to the next gift. That way, it isn't just a madhouse of torn paper flying everywhere without any display of appreciation or gratitude."

Real Advice from Real Moms

"We take our kids to church and tell them the true meaning of Christmas. Then we count how many toys they got for Christmas, and we go through their old toys together and choose the same number to donate to a local charity."

"We tell our children they can each get three gifts for Christmas: one big one and two smaller ones. When the Toys 'R' Us 'Big Toy Book' comes out around Thanksgiving, they spend days analyzing the pages and planning out their three gifts. I believe that makes each gift they receive much more special, and it also saves our house from overwhelming toy clutter!"

- **START SMALL.** Teach your toddler about generosity by encouraging her to share her toys, rewarding her for helping around the house, or showing her how to give a loving hug to someone who is crying or hurt.

- **PRAISE KINDNESS.** When your child does something nice for someone, compliment him. Say, "Thank you for helping Mommy pick up those clothes" or "It's so nice of you to share your book with Timmy."

- **SET AN EXAMPLE.** Let your kids see *you* doing generous acts—even helping an elderly person grab something from a high grocery shelf will make an impression. "If parents do it, children will do it," says Saulitis.

- **TALK ABOUT REACHING OUT.** Slip a newspaper article about a family in need under your child's plate and discuss it over dinner, or direct her attention to causes that spring from the news.

- **GET THEIR INPUT.** By asking your child for her ideas (e.g., "Our neighbor, Mr. Andrews, is sick. What should we do?"), you're saying that her opinions count. "This makes a kid feel valued, which empowers and motivates her," says Saulitis.

- **REMEMBER THE END GOAL.** Showing kids the full circle of their volunteer work makes them want to do more. After your child has collected canned food for the homeless, take her with you to drop it off at the shelter or church so she can see firsthand the results of her work.

- **APPEAL TO THEIR INTERESTS.** Encourage your child to choose an activity that he's passionate about. "Kids love to show what they're good at," explains Saulitis. "And the more you draw on their abilities, the more motivated they become." (See "Volunteer Ideas for Your Child to Try" below for tips.)

Volunteer Ideas for Your Child to Try

CHILDREN WHO LOVE ANIMALS CAN . . .

- Bake dog biscuits or cat treats and deliver them to a local animal shelter. Remember that pets can't eat the same foods as humans, so check for safe recipes before you bake. Or visit the animals to give them much-needed love. (Go to aspca.org to find a shelter near you.)
- Walk or bathe the pet of an elderly or sick neighbor.
- Choose a cow or another animal to buy for a family in a developing country through Heifer International (heifer.org).

CHILDREN WHO LOVE BEING AROUND YOUNGER KIDS CAN . . .

- Teach a young neighbor to ride a bike, tie his shoelaces, or tell time.
- Collect money from family members and take a deserving child to lunch and a holiday play. (Ask your local church for suggestions for whom to take.)
- Tutor younger kids after school.

CHILDREN WHO LOVE NATURE CAN . . .

- Organize a litter patrol for the schoolyard or neighborhood playground.
- Help plant flowers at a local park.
- Cut and arrange fresh flowers and deliver them to patients at a local hospital.

CHILDREN WHO LOVE THE ARTS CAN . . .

- Make holiday greeting cards and give them to the elderly at a senior center.
- Offer to do gift-wrapping for an elderly neighbor or an overstressed new mom.
- Help paint a hospital, shelter, or community-center mural. (Go to artistshelpingchildren.org for local projects.)

CHILDREN WHO LOVE TO READ CAN . . .

- Lead storytimes at libraries and shelters.
- Collect books and magazines from neighbors and deliver them to shelters, day-care centers, and hospitals.
- Read to elderly nursing-home residents who have vision problems.

CHILDREN WHO LOVE INTERACTING WITH PEOPLE CAN . . .

- Visit a convalescent home and take wheelchair-bound patients for walks.
- Go to a homeless shelter and play with the kids who live there.
- Put together simple bag lunches and distribute them to the homeless.
- Organize a canned-food drive at school and prepare and serve food to the homeless at a local church or shelter.

Traditions

Whether you hang stockings at Christmas or go around the table at Thanksgiving stating the one thing you're most grateful for, traditions are often the defining moments or events of the holiday season. Check out the defining moments for real moms below.

Real Advice from Real Moms

What Do You Say When Your Kid Asks if Santa Is Real?

"When my children started asking if Santa was real, my heart broke a little, but my answer is that Santa is not one person with a white beard but everyone in the world who gives freely and loves openly. As a family we have always picked a child in need to share the Christmas spirit with. My kids get a kick out of being Santa for someone else."

Treasured Traditions

Do you have special traditions that you share with your family during the holidays? Try these mom-tested ways of celebrating.

"On Christmas Eve, the kids go outside and sprinkle reindeer food—a mixture of oats, glitter, and sesame seeds—on the ground, making sure to leave an apple for Rudolph!

"On Christmas morning, my parents, grandparents, brothers, and their families all come over to share a breakfast feast of eggs, potatoes, bacon, sausage, tamales, and ham. That way, we all see each other first thing and the rest of the day is free to relax or visit with other relatives."

"I have a box full of scrap paper, ribbons, stickers, old cards, and glitter that I bring out every year so our family can make homemade cards for the holidays."

"We have a reusable Advent calendar, but instead of hiding a treat, I slip in a piece of paper with a family activity idea, like 'Bake cookies for the neighbors' or 'Make popcorn and watch a holiday movie.' We even include one for Mom and Dad to go on a date. It's definitely our four children's favorite holiday activity!"

"Every holiday my mother-in-law had everyone—from kids to adults—sign a table-cloth with their names and the date. Then she embroidered them. It was always fun to look back and see who was there each year!"

How to Take a Perfect Holiday Photo

A photo on a holiday card doesn't need to be formal—or feature matching reindeer sweaters. These tips from photographers will help you create picture-perfect season's greetings.

- **FIND THE RIGHT LIGHT.** Early morning or late afternoon creates a warm glow (rather than the unflattering glare of midday), says C. Taylor Crothers, a New York City–based photographer. If you're indoors, stand between your subjects and a window for a soft effect.

- **HOLD THE PLAID.** "Imagine you're dressing for a nice dinner," suggests Elizabeth Messina, a California-based photographer. Patterns are distracting; aim for solids or simple prints to allow faces to take center stage.

- **CAPTURE THE MOMENT.** "The longer you go, the more cranky people will get," says Crothers. Instead of a formal shoot, try taking pictures in several locations. And just because you're behind the camera doesn't mean you can't crack a grin. The more fun the experience is for you, the more it will translate into photos that look fun and spontaneous, not staged.

- **FOCUS ON FIDGETING.** It's the expressiveness of kids that makes them great photo subjects, reminds Messina. Instead of forcing your kids to smile, give them an activity—like playing with the family pet or working together on a puzzle—to make laughs come naturally.

- **KEEP CLICKING.** "Some of my best images happen between poses," says Messina. Keep things fresh by enlisting someone else to take pictures at the same time. The result? Twice the chance of getting a great shot.

Holiday Card Ideas That Aren't Ho-Hum

Want a holiday card that will pop in a sea of red and green? Try some of these *Redbook* reader tips!

"I choose a day to head to the mall with my girls and take shots of them near all the great holiday decorations and displays. They dress for the season, and we have a blast—not to mention great photos!"

"Last year I had each of my three children hold a wooden letter to spell out the word joy. It turned out so pretty!"

"I take a photo of my sons playing in the snow from the previous year. Or I'll take a picture of them at the beach during the summer, with a "Wish you were here" message."

"My husband and I try to have our card reflect something about who we are, like a photo of us at a Rolling Stones concert or hiking through Yosemite."

CHAPTER NINE

Fun and Games

Life isn't all fun and games—but it should be! So here's great advice on letting kids be kids (including the revolutionary idea of just bumming around), ways to reclaim the lost art of playing with your children, and vital information on friends, sports, travel, vacations, and camp. It'll all help you avoid hassles, save money, and remember why you had kids in the first place!

Play

Here are smart strategies for letting our kids play, and for remembering how to play ourselves.

How to Let Kids Be Kids

There's a good chance that your child is, right now, making his own Harry Potter broomstick out of a stick he found in the backyard . . . and he might prefer it to the pricey vibrating plastic version you were thinking of buying him. Childhood experts and those who have studied the stressed-out are weighing in on the ways we can help our children reclaim simpler pleasures. Here are a few of their suggestions for slowing down and getting a little balance back into kids' lives:

- **EMBRACE THE JOY OF GOOFING AROUND.** If you live in an area where you can let your child run amok with his friends outdoors, let him; if you don't, remember that just hanging with friends and neighbors indoors can be great too.

- **LIMIT KIDS TO ONE OR TWO ACTIVITIES PER SEASON.** Some parents are taking the less-is-more idea a step further, at least temporarily. "One semester we took the girls out of *everything,* says Soledad O'Brien, an anchor and special correspondent for CNN and mother of four children under 8. She then substituted dates with her daughters: Once a week Mom picked up one girl, who got to do whatever she wanted—museum, bookstore, carriage ride in Central Park, lunch in the CNN cafeteria (a favorite). "One-on-one time is great, especially with four kids," says O'Brien. "And a child walking down the street telling complete strangers, 'I'm on a date with my mom!' is really sweet."

What's Your Best Idea for a Low-Cost Birthday Celebration?

"When my youngest son was 4, he loved fire trucks, so we got boxes from the store, paint, and kid-size aprons, then let the kids loose with the material and their imaginations. They created a fire station complete with trucks and ladders. The party was supposed to end at 2, but everyone had so much fun, they stayed till 5!"

"My son loves *Star Wars*, so for his 7th birthday, I sent out invitations asking all the Jedi to come save Princess Leia. I bought inexpensive fabric and made simple tunics and sashes. When the kids arrived at our house, they took turns fighting the 'evil count' (my husband) with a toy lightsaber, and then we shared a *Star Wars* cake. It was so much fun to see all the kids feel like they were on a mission."

"When my youngest turned 5, we set up an obstacle course in the yard. The kids has to move a ball from one bucket to the other, crawl through an expandable nylon tunnel, hop between sticks, and do a forward roll. It was a blast, and we didn't buy a thing!"

- **EAT DINNER TOGETHER.** Forget homework and extracurriculars; if you really want your children to thrive, break bread with them. "For young children, mealtime at home is a stronger predictor of academic achievement and psychological adjustment than time spent in school, studying, sports, church/religious activities, or art activities," says William J. Doherty, Ph.D., a professor of marriage and family therapy at the University of Minnesota and author of *The Intentional Family*. And for older kids? Family dinner is not only a strong predictor of academic success; it is also correlated with lower rates of alcohol and drug use, early sexual behavior, and suicide risk.

- **ENCOURAGE MORE HUMAN TIME, LESS SCREEN AND TOY TIME.** Our children are spending larger and larger chunks of time with *stuff* and less time with people. "Think about it," says David Elkind, Ph.D., whose book *The Power of Play* examines the critical role of unstructured playtime in kids' lives. "Even with something as simple as a car ride . . . parents used to use car time to talk to their kids, and now the kids are watching DVDs in the back seat." Elkind also notes that the reason classic toys like Etch A Sketch, Mr. Potato Head, and Play-Doh are still popular is that they don't direct a child's play; they don't say, "Here's the story. Play with me like this." Instead, these simpler toys allow for more wide-ranging, creative experience.

- **INTRODUCE COMPUTERS WITH CAUTION.** Many childhood experts agree that the interactive quality of computers can be powerfully motivating for kids who are learning to read and write—and games can be just plain pleasurable, too. But, notes Elkind, computers are finding their ways into tinier and tinier hands. "There are these little computers and computer games for 6-month-olds now," he says. "Parents who say, 'Well, computers are part of our world' are right. But to them I say: 'Microwaves are part of our world too, and you wouldn't stick one in the crib of a 6-month-old.'"

FUN AND GAMES

- **RECLAIM SUMMER.** Maybe it's time for all of us to stop thinking of summer vacation as an opportunity to burnish a resume. Children *and* parents need that hiatus to recharge. As a bonus, if you relax over the summer, you're going to be rejuvenated in time for back-to-school.

- **BE OUTNUMBERED.** Jill Davidson, an education writer in Providence, RI, is by nature a planner and a scheduler. But she discovered that the secret to giving her family more unscheduled time was . . . having a bigger family. She recently had a third son, and now "I don't have as much time, energy, or money to drag them around," she says. "I'm with the baby, Leo plays with his trucks in the yard, Elias does endless baseball replays outside and works on his stats, and they both go and play with the neighbors. Since the baby came along, I am paying a little less attention to them. And you know what? They're fine. Better than fine—I think they're happier."

- **LEARN TO TRUST YOUR CHILD.** This may be the most important parenting rule of all, says Elkind. "Children are self-directed learners—they are naturally curious—and how they learn is through play."

Taking Away Toxic Toys

There have been so many recalls lately it feels like you need to don combat gear to clean out your child's toy box. How can a mom keep her kid safe and avoid tantrums when it's time to trash a beloved toy? Follow these tips:

- If your child's favorite toy turns out to be toxic, take it away swiftly yet gently, recommends Jennifer Hartstein, Psy.D. "Accept that there is going to be a meltdown and validate his feelings by saying, 'I understand you're upset, and I'm sorry we have to take it away.'" Don't try to explain to a 2- or 3-year-old that the toy is "sick," Hartstein adds, since they're likely to ask questions about when it will get "better." And you can always divert a kid's attention with a new, nontoxic toy as a replacement.

- Ask your pediatrician to test your children for lead at ages 1 and 2 and make sure they're getting enough calcium and iron, since a lack of these minerals causes the body to absorb more lead.

- Keep up-to-date on the latest recalls at cpsc.gov.

How to Play with Your Kids

You make sure the piano is practiced and the homework is done—and then your husband comes home, spends 10 minutes playing "dinosaur vs. Jedi," and he's known as the "fun one." Well, Mom can be just as big a barrel of laughs; the only one stopping you is *you*. Ann Pleshette Murphy, author of *The Secret of Play,* shares how to clown around with your kids—while getting everything else done too.

Make over the witching hour.
You know that time around 6 p.m. when you're trying to get dinner on the table, your kids are whining, and everyone is ready to explode? Push dinner back 15 minutes—instead, give the kids a quick snack and play a game of Sorry, or just tickle each other on the couch and make goofy jokes, says Murphy. "We think a good mom has to come home, drop her briefcase or groceries, and jump into the kitchen right away," she says. "But the kids are melting down because they're craving a connection with you."

Giggle while you work.
Murphy points out that for a young child, vacuuming, sorting the silverware, helping roll meatballs, or even setting the table can be a blast as long as it's done with the right attitude (e.g., leave your micromanaging tendencies at the office). Sing or boogie together while you're working, and don't criticize her efforts. Upbeat time together is more important than a perfectly folded napkin.

Don't be afraid to be silly.
You don't have to be Lucille Ball to make your kids laugh. Talk in a silly voice, stick a pair of pajama pants on your head when you're getting them ready for bed, or make up a lame knock-knock joke. "Inherent in being a playful parent is being willing to make a fool of yourself once in a while," says Murphy. So go ahead—be a fool for love.

Friends

Sometimes a child needs a little help making a friend, and sometimes she needs help patching up a friendship after a fight. Try the tips below to help your child with both.

Friends Aren't Just for Fun

Having friends may be as important to your child's health as nutritious foods and getting enough sleep, according to a study from the Institute of Psychiatry in London. Researchers there found that socially isolated kids—ones who preferred to do things on their own or weren't well liked—were about one-and-a-half-times more likely than other kids to experience health problems such as cardiovascular disease as adults. To help your child avoid the risks of extreme loneliness, "it's important to encourage social interaction as early as the preschool years," says Avshalom Caspi, Ph.D., lead author of the study.

- If your child is shy, arrange one-on-one playdates at your house, where he'll be more at ease.
- Don't push him to interact with groups if he's not comfortable, but encourage him to develop at least one close pal. "It's not how many friends your child has that matters, but the quality of those friendships," says Caspi.
- Don't worry if your child seems to enjoy more alone time than other kids. "That's normal," says Caspi. "It's the chronic and pervasive social isolation that should signal concern." If you feel that your child suffers from chronic isolation, talk to your pediatrician.

Real Advice from Real Moms

How Do You Teach Your Child to Be a Good Friend?

"My daughter is very social, and she's at that age when her friends are on a revolving loop—I never know who's in and who's out. When she's down in the dumps because a girl at school doesn't like her, I'll ask her about another girl who I've noticed she's treated poorly. I comfort her too, but I want her to truly be aware of her responsibility: Being a good friend is more valuable than any amount of popularity."

What Do You Do When Your Child Has a Fight with a Friend?

"I want my son to know I'm always here for him, but also that he needs to figure things out for himself, so I give him examples of fights I had with friends when I was a kid and how we resolved it. I hope he can use my examples to work it out on his own."

"I calmly ask, 'How did the fight start?' 'Why do you think your friend did that?' 'What did you do?' 'What would have been a better choice?' It's important for my kids to understand that they have the power and the responsibility to avoid and correct these situations."

"When my 5-year-old daughter has a fight with her buddy, I ask her how she feels, tell her that her friend is feeling the same, and that she should say she's sorry and ask for a do-over."

Sports

Whether your child is a natural athlete or a tangle of limbs who spends most of his time on the bench, you need to take pay close attention to what he says about his sport. What do you do if he complains that he's sore? What do you do if she wants to quit the team? And how do you pick out a bike, the quintessential kid exercise machine? The answers are below.

Are Your Child's Aches Serious?

You want your young athlete to play hard, but watch out: Overuse injuries that develop subtly over time are on the rise, according to data from the National Athletic Trainers' Association (NATA), and they could stall or end your child's athletic "career" if they're left untreated. The sports most likely to cause such injuries: baseball, basketball, dance, cheerleading, and martial arts.

How can you spot an overuse injury?

"Look for soreness that doesn't get better by the next morning," says Chuck Kimmel, former president of NATA. "Or, the next time she plays, if she immediately starts hurting again, she should see a doctor."

How can you prevent these injuries?

A good warm-up can help prevent overuse injuries, as will icing any sore spots. And make sure your child isn't overdoing it on the field: Have her stick to about two practices and one game a week, each for no more than an hour and 15 minutes.

Get Rolling: Choosing a Bike

Your child's first bike is more than just a big toy: "For a 6-, 7-, or 8-year old, it means freedom," says Patrick McCormick, of the League of American Bicyclists. Here's how to pick a bike you and your kid will *both* feel good about:

- **GET A BIKE THAT FITS YOUR KID *NOW*.** A lot of parents choose one that's a little too big so there's room to grow, but that may mean your child can't ride it safely.
- **CHECK THE BRAKES.** Coaster brakes, which you activate by pedaling backward, may be easier and safer than hand brakes.
- **BUY A BELL OR HORN,** since most bikes come unequipped. (Would you want to drive without a horn?)
- **LET YOUR CHILD PICK A HELMET THAT LOOKS "COOL,"** so she'll like it enough to wear it. That said, make sure her choice has been okayed by the Consumer Product Safety Commission (the CPSC seal

should be inside the helmet) and fits snugly, with no more than two inches' clearance between the bridge of your child's nose and the helmet's base.

When Kids Want to Quit

He begged you to let him take up hockey. Then, after a few weeks, your child announces that he wants to quit. Do you say okay or make him stick it out? Jeanne Brockmyer, a clinical child psychologist and professor at the University of Toledo, offers advice.

- **LOOK AT THE CALENDAR.** "If your kid is over-committed, he can't be expected to maintain enthusiasm for a new activity," says Funk. "One sport plus one arts or scout activity at a time is more than enough for a grade-schooler."

- **LISTEN TO HIS COMPLAINTS WITH EMPATHY.** Say, "It can be really hard to get going with something new," Funk suggests. Remind him of past situations where activities started out rocky but worked out well— whether it was for him, a sibling, or even yourself.

- **SET SOME TERMS.** If your child just seems to lack motivation, say that he must keep going for four or five more practices. He can withdraw if he's still unhappy, but there should be a consequence, such as extra chores.

- **GET A SECOND OPINION.** "Talk to the coach and get his perception of your child's participation, talent, and likely reason for not wanting to continue," says Funk. Kids are more apt to keep up activities that showcase their strengths, so let him do things he really enjoys.

Travel

Packing, driving, flying . . . travel can be exhausting for adults. But when you throw kids into the mix, you can *all* end up tired and frustrated. Here's what you need to know to make the trip go smoothly.

Hassle-free Air Travel

Traveling with kids is tricky enough, but add strict security measures and crowded airports and you've got a recipe for trouble. Follow this expert advice for smoother sailing in the skies.

- **TIRE OUT YOUR TRAVELERS.** Ask airport personnel whether there's a place for your kids to release some pent-up energy. "Some airports have play areas just for kids," says Kari Thomas, president of Will Travel, a family-oriented travel agency in Bucks County, PA. If you have to take a connecting flight, book one with plenty of time between legs so your children can run around a little before being buckled back in.
- **TRAVEL DURING OFF-PEAK HOURS.** "Midday flights are your best bet because they aren't as busy as early-morning ones, yet they're usually not as delayed as later flights," says Thomas.
- **RESERVE YOUR SEATS.** Avoid the bulkhead—these seats may offer more legroom, but you can't stash items under them, like a bag of toys.
- **ASK THE AIRLINE FOR PERMISSION TO PRE-BOARD YOUR FAMILY.** Many airlines will let families with young children board the plane first.

Real Advice from Real Moms

How Do You Keep Everyone Entertained During a Long Car Trip?

"I pack each kid's favorite snack in a separate bag. I try to be prepared with wipes, books they haven't seen before, water, trash bags—probably too much stuff, but better safe than sorry!"

How Do You Keep Everyone Entertained During a Long Car Trip?

"We play Horses and Graveyards. Everyone counts how many horses they spot as we drive along, and they earn points for each horse. Then the first person to spot a graveyard shouts out, 'Graveyard!' which wipes out everyone else's horse totals. The kids love this game. They continually scan the countryside, and that often brings up other conversations about the scenery."

"I'm not proud of it, but we survive long car rides with portable DVD players, iPods, Leapsters, and Game Boys. How did we ever do it without them?"

Traveling with Tots? How to Pack

By the time you pack up the million different games, toys, books, swim goggles, stuffed animals, strollers, jackets, swimsuits, and portable cribs that your kids need for a week away in a warm climate, there may not be enough room left for your makeup bag. But it *is* possible to get into the car or on the plane without 62 different pieces of baggage. Here's what you really need for a fun family vacation and what you can leave behind.

Clothes

For most trips, your kids don't need anything fancier than a sundress or a polo shirt. Pack just one outfit per kid, per day—you can always hand-wash little spills and spots if necessary. "To make it easy for the kids to get dressed, pack entire outfits—socks, underwear, shorts, and shirt—in Ziploc bags," advises Susan Foster, author of *Smart Packing for Today's Traveler.* "At the end of the day, the dirties can go back in the bags." Be sure to bring one pair of long pants and one long-sleeve shirt for cooler evenings, a fleece sweatshirt (great for layering), and a rain poncho or Windbreaker. Have everyone wear sneakers on the plane, pack sandals and water shoes, and you're done.

Gear

Look for multifunction items, like a car seat/stroller, suggests Foster. Or leave your SUV-size stroller at home and bring an inexpensive umbrella type that's easier to fold and carry. If you're flying, check out babysaway.com—they rent cribs, strollers, exersaucers, and more, and will have them waiting in your hotel room when you get there. Also, check with your car rental agency: Most will provide a car seat for a few dollars per day.

FUN AND GAMES

Entertainment

"Give each child a backpack and let them take whatever books and toys can fit in it," Foster suggests. Leave home any games with lots of pieces, hardcover books, and large toys. Stock up on sticker books, card games, mini Play-Doh packs, and crayons (and keep a few surprises in your own bag to pull out when they get antsy).

Don't Leave Home Without . . .

Prescriptions, diapers, and wipes (unless there's a drugstore near your hotel), lots of snacks and drinks—and, of course, that can't-sleep-without-it teddy or blankie.

Vacation

Whether your summer consists of the kids going away to camp, the family taking a trip to a theme park, quiet time reading, or an adults-only vacation, you'll find invaluable advice here's some from experts and moms alike.

Grown-ups-only Getaways

Imagine a vacation filled with romantic dinners (instead of McDonald's stops) and leisurely strolls on the beach (instead of hours at the water park). Sounds heavenly, doesn't it? Yet 32 percent of parents surveyed by travel Web site kayak.com have *never* gone on a vacation sans children. "It's emotionally refreshing for parents to take a kid-free vacation," says Eileen Ogintz, creator of takingthekids.com. "You can focus on your relationship, and it's good for the kids too: It fosters their sense of independence." If you find yourself gazing wistfully at brochures of adults-only resorts, here's how to make your fantasy vacation happen.

**When You
Can't Afford a Big
Family Trip, How
Do You Bring
the Vacation
Fun Home?**

"We live in the suburbs of Cleveland but don't make it into the city often. So on a recent staycation, I ditched the car and took my three kids and their friends into downtown Cleveland on the rapid transit to visit the science center. It was a thrill for them to go on the train with their friends, and it really helped them see their own city in a whole different way."

Keep your kids in a comfy place.

This is not the time to try out a new sitter or send them for their first sleepover at their grandmother's, says Ogintz. Either plan an overnight trial at Grandma's a few weeks *before* your trip, or have a loved and trusted sitter come stay at your house while you're gone. And start slowly: Think a weekend at a nearby inn rather than two weeks in Tahiti.

Make it as exciting for the kids as it is for you.

While you're gone, have the sitter take them to a ball game or a movie they've been dying to see, or schedule playdates with their best friends.

Define your time away.

Give kids a concrete way to count off the days by marking them on a calendar or giving them a card to open each day. "One mom I know puts aside a pair of socks for each day she's gone," says Ogintz. "When her child is on the last pair, she knows that means Mom is coming home."

Tell yourself it's okay.

More than 80 percent of the mothers in the kayak.com survey said they would feel at least some guilt on their adults-only vacation (interestingly, far fewer dads felt guilty). To help with that, buy some fun souvenirs for the kids and vow to be a little more patient with them when you get home. Then sit back, sip that umbrella drink, and enjoy.

Rest, Relaxation, and Reading

Summer is the perfect time to cultivate your child's love for books. How can you help him see reading as fun instead of as off-season schoolwork? Carol Brey-Casiano, former president of the American Library Association, offers some pointers.

- **MAKE SURE HE HAS HIS OWN LIBRARY CARD.** "It's often the first card a child has, and it's that first step to independence, making library trips more special."
- **CREATE A COMFORTABLE READING SPACE AT HOME.** Set up a spot in his room—maybe a dedicated beanbag—with a shelf or a crate where he can keep his latest book selections.
- **MAKE THE MOST OF DRIVE TIME.** On road trips, let him pick out some audio books for the ride so the entire family can listen together and talk about them afterward. Some kids' audio books come with companion print versions, Brey-Casiano notes, so kids can follow along on the page.

Theme Park Survival: Stop the Meltdowns

Roller coasters! Bumper cars! Cotton candy! What kid doesn't love a trip to a theme park? All that excitement, though, can lead to tears. "There's a lot of hurry-up-and-wait with lines, and kids feel like they have no control," says child-development expert Lea Ann Browning McNee, Outreach and Development Officer at the National Council for Community Behavioral Healthcare. Here's how to prevent a tantrum.

- **PLAN FOR DOWNTIME.** Slyly work in breaks between attractions—find sit-down moments, such as indoor shows, that coincide with your child's usual naptimes.
- **SCOPE OUT TOYS AND TREATS.** Instead of negotiating treats at every snack stand, ask your child to pick out the two she wants most over the course of the day. And let her choose a souvenir early, before she's exhausted—then buy it on the way out so it won't get wet or lost.
- **MAKE LINES FUN.** Bring an activity book, or "have her count people in red shirts—anything to make waiting in line not feel like waiting in line," says Browning McNee.

Real Advice from Real Moms

When You Can't Afford a Big Family Trip, How Do You Bring the Vacation Fun Home?

"I let my kids look at a globe or map and decide where in the whole world they would like to 'visit.' Then we'll do an art project related to that country, download some native music from iTunes, and prepare snacks from that country. It's great fun, and it teaches them about a whole different culture."

"We're throwing a beach party in our house this winter! First we'll make some ocean-themed crafts to decorate the boys' room, then we'll mix up some fruit smoothies and dance around to the Beach Boys' music.

GET ONE-ON-ONE TIME. If you can, plan for each kid to get an hour alone with a grown-up. "The child gets to be the center of attention, which helps her feel like she's not working to be heard above the excitement," says Browning McNee. "That is incredibly reenergizing."

Battling the Homesick Blues

Got a child heading to sleepaway camp? Christopher Thurber, Ph.D., school psychologist at Phillips Exeter Academy and coauthor of *The Summer Camp Handbook,* offers these tips for handling homesickness.

Plan for it.
Research shows that talking about homesickness helps prevent it. "Say, 'Hey, whenever people are away from home, they miss things, so let's talk about what you do when that happens,'" Thurber suggests.

Have an upbeat send-off.
"Don't say, 'I don't know what we'll do without you,'" says Thurber. It can make your child feel anxious. Tell her you'll miss her, and emphasize what a great time she's going to have."

Keep in touch—but not by phone.
"A parent's voice is all it takes to turn normal feelings of homesickness into a tidal wave of longing," says Thurber. Write letters instead.

Don't cave if she begs to come home.
Try to let your child work through her feelings so that she gains self-reliance. If she does come home early, discuss what was good about the stay—which will build a great foundation for trying again next summer.

Index

Library of Congress Cataloging-in-Publication Data
Mom's survival guide : real wisdom from real moms to save time, money, and sanity / the editors of Redbook Magazine. -- 1st pbk. ed.
    p. cm.
Includes index.
ISBN 978-1-58816-804-7
1. Motherhood. 2. Mothers. 3. Child rearing. 4. Parenting. I. Redbook. II. Title: Redbook mom's survival guide.
HQ759.M8475 2010
649'.10852--dc22
                    2009026579

10 9 8 7 6 5 4 3 2 1

Published by Hearst Books
A division of Sterling Publishing Co., Inc.
387 Park Avenue South, New York, NY 10016

Redbook is a registered trademark of Hearst Communications, Inc.

www.redbookmag.com

For information about custom editions, special sales, premium and corporate purchases, please contact Sterling Special Sales Department at 800-805-5489 or specialsales@sterlingpublishing.com.

Distributed in Canada by Sterling Publishing
c/o Canadian Manda Group, 165 Dufferin Street
Toronto, Ontario, Canada M6K 3H6

Distributed in Australia by Capricorn Link (Australia) Pty. Ltd.
P.O. Box 704, Windsor, NSW 2756 Australia

Printed in USA

Sterling ISBN 978-1-58816-804-7